The Downside Prayerbook

The Downside Prayerbook

Edited by David Foster
Foreword by Cardinal Basil Hume
Preface by Timothy Radcliffe OP

burns & oates

BURNS & OATES

A Continuum Imprint
The Tower Building, 11 York Rd, London SE1 7NX
80 Maiden Lane, Suite 704, New York, NY 10038
www.continuumbooks.com

First published in 1999
Second edition published in 2003
Paperback edition published in 2005
Reprinted 2009

ISBN: PB: 978-0-86012-418-4

British Library Cataloguing-in-Publication Data
A catalogue record for this book is available from the British Library

Designed by Derek Birdsall RDI
Typeset by Omnific
Printed and bound in Great Britain by CPI Antony Rowe

Contents

Foreword

One of the most important things we can do in life is to learn the habit of daily prayer. Daily prayer shapes our understanding of each day, strengthens us in moments of difficulty, guides us in moments of decision and is a comfort to us in moments of distress.

The earlier in life we learn the habit of prayer the better. The family circle is, of course, the best school of prayer. There we can learn of the love which God has for each one of us, and how we can respond to that love, each day, with prayers of thankfulness and praise.

The habit of prayer, like all habits, is built up by repetition. We learn to love the prayers we say often. We learn the ways of prayer which suit us best. We learn of the riches contained in the tradition of the Church. That tradition is, indeed, a treasury of prayer.

I welcome this publication: *The Catholic Prayerbook from Downside Abbey*. It contains hints on how to pray, on how to prepare for the celebration of the sacraments. It contains prayers for Morning, Evening and Night-time, prayers to use before the Blessed Sacrament and prayers in praise of Mary. It presents prayers from many sources and for many occasions. It is truly Catholic. I am sure that all who use this prayerbook will find in it inspiration and assistance.

The need for us to be people of prayer has never been more urgent. We know that unless we are deeply rooted in a sense of God's presence and able to refer all things to God then our pilgrimage into the future will be marked more by uncertainty than by the peace which is God's gift.

Cardinal Basil Hume
Archbishop of Westminster

Preface

I welcome this new prayerbook from Downside Abbey because
I think that it will be of help to people like me who find it hard to
pray. The idea of praying is very attractive, but once I begin then so
often I am bored, distracted, and my feet itch to be anywhere else.

How can this book of prayers be a help? It mainly consists of other
people's prayers. There are the prayers of men and women, the old and
the young, people who are alive today and others who died thousands
of years ago, foreigners and English people, scholars and peasants.
What help are other people's words when I speak to God? Is not real
prayer spontaneous, when I use my own words to talk to my Creator?
The story is told of a priory of English Dominicans during the last
World War – and I am sure other religious Orders have versions of this
story. The brethren were said to have been singing Vespers when they
heard the sound of enemy bombers overhead. In a moment of panic
the Prior shouted, 'Brothers, stop saying Vespers and start praying!'
What did he think that they had been doing until then?

These prayers can help me to pray, because they teach me the
language of friendship. All prayer is talking to God as to a friend, and
it is God's closest friends who can teach me how to do that best. When
we fall in love for the first time and make a passionate declaration
to the beloved, then it is unlikely that our words are very original.
They are probably borrowed words, that we have picked up from the
television or a film, from the latest novel we have read. It takes time
for us to discover our own voice, our own words. And so it is when
we talk to God. We begin by using the words of those people who
have been his friends, above all the saints, and thus learn, slowly,
how to speak to God with the words of true friendship.

Also, when we use other people's words in prayer, we are
reminded that we are not alone. Other people have lived through our
failures, our wild hopes and fears, our sorrows and our joys and they
are with us as we pray.

When Dietrich Bonhoeffer spent his last night in a concentration
camp before he was executed by the Nazis, he prayed, 'O God, in the
early morning I cry to you. Help me to pray and to concentrate my

thoughts on you: I cannot do this alone'. We face the challenges of life and death with all the rest of God's friends at our side, and so it is right that we use their words too.

The wonderful prayers in this book teach us two other vital things about friendship with God. The first is confidence in God's presence. When we pray we may wonder whether anyone is there. Here we are, begging for help, but is anyone listening? We may feel as if we are sending e-mails into galactic cyberspace, but does anyone open the mail? These prayers are filled with the confidence that prayer is not crying out to an absent God, because God has already come to us. Prayer is not about making contact with God, but about welcoming God who is already present and is just waiting for the chance to come into my life. 'Behold, I stand at the door and knock; if any one hears my voice and opens the door, I will come in to him and eat with him, and he with me' (Revelation 3.20).

Secondly, if we pray we come to see that our lives are filled with gifts. We live in a society which does not believe in a 'free lunch'. Everything must be earned and paid for. And indeed the value of everything is the price that it fetches in the market. But prayer teaches that this is not how things really are, because everything is a gift from God: my friends, happiness, food and drink, success, love, beauty, my very life, even the moments of suffering.

G. K. Chesterton once wrote that every Christmas morning he awoke and gave thanks for the presents from God in the stockings at the foot of his bed, his own legs. Reading the prayers in this book is an education in gratitude.

This book contains prayers for every moment of the day and year, and for every crisis that we can ever face, from passing exams to facing death. Prayer is not a special hermetically sealed part of our lives, any more than friendship can be part-time. It comes to penetrate all that we do and are.

May this book help all those who use it to grow in God's friendship and open our eyes to his unimaginable generosity.

Timothy Radcliffe OP
Former Master of the Order of Preachers

Introduction

With Voice and Mind and Heart

Prayer is the language of our friendship with God, and we learn this language as we learn all other languages, by practice with the vocabulary and grammar of prayer. A difficulty with the language of prayer is that God is a very different kind of conversation partner from other friends. We do not see him or hear him with the bodily senses and he has no ears or eyes to see and listen to us. That does not mean that there is no point in using prayers like the ones in this book. It means that there is more to praying than just using words, although for us the words are an essential first step in this further process of learning how to grow in the art of communication with God.

Talking with anyone, in fact, always means more than words. The words only express a meaning which involves the mind. Both understanding and thought are needed, and feelings and intentions are also part of a conversation; both of these reflect our hopes and desires, and say a great deal about what we love and how we use our capacity for love. For the same reasons prayer involves not only 'prayers', like the ones in this book: it involves not only words but also our minds and our hearts. As you use this book, try to let the prayers teach you how to use your own words to express your thoughts and desires to God. They are offered as guides in the language of prayer, suggestions for the vocabulary and grammar used in talking with God and growing in a personal knowledge of him.

We live in a busy world and there are not many pointers towards God in our daily lives which make it easy for us to find him. The prayers which form such a rich part of the Christian tradition can often help by providing a framework and guidance for our imagination and thoughts as we try to find the way to the place in our hearts where prayer comes more freely of itself. Let these prayers touch our hearts and open them up to God.

Suggestions are given throughout the book for how to make good use of the various opportunities there are to pray. There are introductions and practical guidelines as well as a choice of prayers to help you pray for yourself.

There are various ways of using the prayers:

1. Slow reading: Choose a prayer to read slowly and quietly. Make the words and thoughts of the prayer your own in whatever way seems best, for example, thinking about their meaning and how it applies to you, or expanding on their ideas in a more personal way, praying for particular people or things. Always remember you are in God's presence and you are sharing time with him and talking to him.

2. Points of departure: Sometimes a few words are enough to start us praying in our own words. The prayers just help to put us in the presence of God, on his wavelength, as it were. Never let the words become a chain that prevents you freely responding to God. But that chain can become an anchor: the words can keep us focused on prayer rather than wandering off in daydreams or all sorts of thinking which takes us away from God. When we find we have drifted away, we can return to the prayer and let it bring us back to the point of what we are trying to do.

3. Fall backs: Sometimes we cannot pray. Perhaps we are ill, tired, or fed up; perhaps we are in a dark patch on the road to God. These are times when we can find our faith, hope and love strengthened by the prayers of others. We need never be ashamed to use other people's prayers when we have not got anything of our own to say.

Prayer is not private property and people who pray cannot pretend their prayers are their own and no one else's – or that no one else's will do as well. Sometimes the prayers of other people are much better; they say just what we would want to say better than we ever could. We belong to a great family which is united in prayer and we always depend on the prayer of others, especially of the saints and holy people who inspire us. We certainly depend on Jesus who prays for us and teaches us to pray. The real prayer is always what God is praying in us through the Holy Spirit; we have to find whatever way we can to unite ourselves to that.

This is a book you can always keep with you. Let the prayers in it teach you different ways of praying for yourself all through your life. Use them in whatever way helps you to find your own contact with God, and let yourself stay as quietly as possible in his presence.

Acts of Prayer

Using prayers by other people helps us talk to God in our own thoughts and words. But as we get into the habit of praying for ourselves the words and the thoughts will probably become less important (at any rate some of the time) than just being there in God's presence. We learn that the praying goes on behind or below the conscious activity of our minds. That is why silence is an essential part of prayer for many people. Silence gives us the inner space we need to search for God in our prayers. In the quietness of that space we can begin to reach down into our hearts.

For prayer really goes on in our hearts. Jesus said that it was from the heart that our thoughts, desires and attitudes come, good and bad, which give our lives their spiritual colour and shape. Prayer helps us open our hearts to God so that he can heal and strengthen us by the Holy Spirit. The heart is our spiritual centre. It is where God touches us and, if we live by faith, hope and love, the heart becomes the place where he dwells. It is holy ground.

This book contains different kinds of prayer and each of them can teach us something different about our relationship with God. When we are learning to pray it is good to get to know each of these kinds of prayer and practice them because they help us explore for ourselves the various ways our lives are lived towards God. We can get a general picture of this if we think in terms of five kinds of prayer. The traditional names for these kinds are: adoration, confession, thanksgiving, intercession and supplication.

Adoration

To adore God means simply letting God be God, praising him for who and what he is. This is the simplest and deepest kind of prayer, and all prayer eventually turns towards adoration of God; but it is a good way to start praying, putting oneself into his presence.

Confession

When we have put ourselves in God's presence we begin to see ourselves in relationship to him and to see how we fall short of the life he has given us and wants us to live to the full. Not only can we think about specific sins but also about our sinfulness and weakness. Prayer helps us do so in hope and trust, full of faith in God's love.

The first two kinds of prayer explore God and self as honestly and humbly as we can. Sometimes that is all we need to do to pray. But other kinds of prayer explore the way God relates to us through our lives, and by his presence in the world. There are things to look back on thankfully; and needs that call for his action (and ours!).

Thanksgiving

We consider the things God has given us, his gift of life, and the good things that have given us a sense of delight in that life. Everybody likes to be thanked and this is the best way to deepen our friendship with God, to learn to trust and hope in him. We never thank God enough, and as we grow in our faith we can begin to live thankfully even through difficult times where our understanding of God and sense of his presence are tested. We live from God to God and it is from appreciating God's generosity that we learn how to give ourselves to others and to him.

Intercession

We should love our neighbour as ourselves, and we can never love God in isolation from the rest of mankind or the needs of the whole world. On the contrary, a prayerful person will naturally tend to look at the world in God's company and try to see things from God's point of view. In praying for other people we naturally pray for those closest to us – we are immediately responsible for them; but we should try to pray as best we can for the needs of the whole world, and to seek God's will in prayer for other people and situations. In that way we will be able to unite our love to God's own love for others, and that can help God use us to do something through our own concern for them.

Supplication

Jesus wants us to pray for our own needs, and to be as simple and honest about them as we can; he tells us never to give up praying for our needs. Of course God knows what they are and will give us things even before we ask (another reason to be very thankful in prayer). But we are not as gifted with insight as God. If we keep at this kind of prayer we can learn to understand more clearly what our real needs are (ultimately a need for God), and to ask for the things which please him. That is how we can bring our hearts and minds closer to God and live more fully the life he wants for us.

'Acts of prayer' is a traditional phrase used to describe prayer as something we do (an action) however we do it, whether with words, thoughts, or silence. In fact, the phrase 'Prayer of Acts' has been used to refer to the kind of praying which goes on when we use words and thought less and less in our prayer. This is not as odd as it sounds; it is natural for friends to value time spent together however they spend it, and what is important is the quality of the time spent, the attentiveness and generosity shown to each other. In our prayer too we learn that the words are in the end only a way of expressing something much more important. It is usual for people to discover this in silence. You give God the chance simply to be there for you and for you to be there for him. This is the beginning of an even deeper journey in prayer, for which the mystical writers of the Christian Tradition can give the necessary help.

Prayer in Faith, Hope and Love

When we begin to pray, putting ourselves in the presence of God and trying to let God fill our minds and hearts, we should not be surprised if it takes a bit of time to find him. Our hearts and minds are very busy places! But if we are looking for God, we must always remember that God is looking out for us, and is ready to welcome us when we turn to him. If prayer were only a matter of our thoughts, something which went on just in our heads, it would be a cold activity. Prayer involves a search for God who is himself always present in our hearts. It grows out of our faith in that presence. God is the most central, deepest reality in our lives, because we would not exist without him; prayer also expresses our faith in Jesus who has given us a share in God's life by the gift of the Holy Spirit. Besides faith, prayer also expresses our hope in his promises and our appreciation of his love. Hope and love bring our faith to life; they turn it into prayer and make it a living power in our lives.

We can only find God by means of faith, hope and love. That is how, in this life, we relate to him. Acts of faith, hope and love have therefore been among the traditional prayers of Christians, and you will find some of them in this book. They are prayers we need at every stage of our life, because we will always need to renew our faith, hope and love in God. This is specially the case at times of uncertainty and difficulty, when we feel we are lost in the dark on unfamiliar ground. This does not mean that God has disappeared or that he is any further away than before. It means that he is leading us on to find him in a new way in our lives. Sometimes we are being asked to let go of something which has become an obstacle on the journey; sometimes God wants to teach us something new about himself. Either way, these are times of growth in his friendship, times when we will feel very unsure of ourselves, but also times when we can learn to trust and hope in God's love as we have never done before.

Above all we must never despair: we have to travel by day and by night on the path to God and the road has many twists and turns. As we get used to the journey of prayer, we can even begin to prefer the darker times. For these are the times when we have to rely on God rather than ourselves, and we know how unreliable we are. We should try to remember what St Benedict teaches, that all the time we look for God, God is already looking out for us, calling out, inviting us to follow him. God shows us the way to find him, and to find happiness in his presence.

1: Basic Prayers

The Sign of the Cross

The Church begins all its prayer with this sign: it is the sign of our salvation by Jesus Christ's death on the Cross, but it is a sign of power not of defeat, a sign of his victory over death, and his power to give life to all who turn to him. It is used to mark each of God's children for Baptism; it is used at the start of every Mass as a sign of Jesus' presence among us; it is used to give the assurance of his forgiveness in Confession, of his healing in the Sacrament of the Sick, of his undying love when we depart this life to be with him for ever.

When we make the sign of the cross on ourselves we make our own the life and love of Jesus who died and rose again for us. It is a prayer which involves both the body and the spirit. We do not only think of Jesus, but with our hands touch our head, our arms and our heart with the cross. We bring our whole lives, our minds, our bodies and our will and emotions, into contact with his power. The vertical and horizontal arms of the cross express the height and depth of God's love, and its breadth which reaches out through us to make our lives more like his. It also expresses the basic orientation of our lives which we live between heaven and earth, our arms reaching out for fellowship with each other.

As we make the sign of the cross we place ourselves under the power of God the Trinity.

**In the name of the Father and of the Son
and of the Holy Spirit.**

Amen.

A person's name is not just a label. It stands for the real person and
in the Bible the name often tells you who they really are. Jesus,
for example, was given the name which meant 'God saves'. It is a
privilege to know a person's name; calling someone by name claims
their attention; it opens up a relationship with them. Jesus has given
us the power to become children of God; he has given us a share in
his divine nature. So when we pray we use God's name for ourselves,
the name of the Trinity, Father, Son and Holy Spirit.

For through Jesus we come to know God as our own heavenly Father
and are filled with the Holy Spirit which moves us to pray and live
God's life in our own world. Through the Holy Spirit we are not
only disciples of Jesus, but also united with him as parts of his body.
Through sharing the human life of Jesus, we come to rediscover
what it means to be human, to reflect the image of God the creator;
through Jesus we come to know God as the eternal Father, who is
always turned towards us in love, and we are drawn into the mystery
of God which we begin to explore when we pray. But the Sign of the
Cross reminds us that our vocation to be human does not only call us
upwards, as it were, into God; it is a vocation to mankind and indeed
to the whole creation – to be servants of all, and stewards of all that
God has made.

The Lord's Prayer

**Our Father,
who art in heaven,
hallowed be thy name;
thy kingdom come;
thy will be done on earth as it is in heaven.
Give us this day our daily bread;
and forgive us our trespasses
as we forgive those who trespass against us;
and lead us not into temptation;
but deliver us from evil.**

*Pater noster, qui es in cælis,
sanctificetur nomen tuum;
adveniat regnum tuum;
fiat voluntas tua, sicut in cælo, et in terra.
Panem nostrum cotidianum da nobis hodie;
et dimitte nobis debita nostra,
sicut et nos dimittimus debitoribus nostris;
et ne nos inducas in tentationem;
sed libera nos a malo.*

The Lord's prayer has always been taught as a pattern for prayer.
It is the prayer Jesus used to teach his disciples how to pray.

The basic shape of the prayer teaches us that prayer should begin
with God and then turn to our own needs as well as to our
relationships with others, and it ends by turning to our basic need
for protection and strength in the face of temptation and evil.

Each line in the prayer can be used as a starting point for meditation
about the meaning of prayer.

Our Father

Prayer begins by turning our whole attention to God.
But he is not remote from us:
our whole existence depends on him:
in him we live and move and have our being.
Without his presence in the depth of our heart,
we would simply cease to exist.
He is always there, waiting for us, loving us as a Father,
full of love and compassion.
He created us: he has given us life, talents and everything we have.
We are his own children and reflect in our lives
something unique about him.
We are not our own; we belong to God as children whom he loves.
This makes everyone our brothers and sisters;
no one can be excluded from our concern.

who art in heaven

Heaven is where we should be aiming all our lives,
for that is where God lives purely and wholly from all eternity.
God is in the depths of our hearts, but he is also the goal of our lives,
our happiness and joy.
We live from God to God.
When we turn to him, our first prayer is one of praise and adoration
simply letting God be God.

hallowed be thy name

We turn to God in thanksgiving and blessing for all he has given us,
for his presence in our lives and world.
God is never absent, even where it is hard to find him,
even in the midst of evil, where human hearts,
are turned away from him by sin.
Prayer draws us into the mystery of God,
the mystery of his power and love,
the mystery of his holiness.

thy kingdom come

Our prayer is also one of desire for him,
an attraction to him at the heart of the mystery of our own lives:
our deepest desire is for him,
when we know ourselves as fully as God knows us.
Prayer also responds to the world's need for him,
for his peace and justice.

thy will be done on earth as it is in heaven

In prayer we commit ourselves to God,
and offer ourselves to him as free human beings,
with all the powers he has given us to live here and now
the life we hope to enjoy for ever with him in heaven.
Prayer is utterly practical.
By praying we seek to understand the world,
and our own lives as God sees them,
to love as he loves, to want as he wants,
and to live accordingly.

Give us this day our daily bread

So we pray for ourselves,
for what we really need in order to live according to God's will:
we pray for basic needs – for others' needs too;
we pray for today not for tomorrow.
God is here and now:
prayer is about the real world, not about wishful thinking.

and forgive us our trespasses

One of our real needs is forgiveness.
Our sins damage ourselves most of all,
because they damage the most important friendship of our lives,
our friendship with God.
Repentance helps us begin the work of reconciliation
in human relationships
by helping us find healing and peace in our own hearts,
something we can share with others in intercession.
Repentance is the foundation of true prayer for the world.

as we forgive those who trespass against us

Real prayer makes a difference to the way we live;
it expresses itself in action.
Repentance means letting go of grievances, a new openness to others.
Through the conversion of our lives
we help turn the world back to God.
Prayer reshapes the programme of our lives.

and lead us not into temptation

As we look towards the challenge of living faithfully,
prayerfully we face up to our weakness and limitations,
and trust in God to guide us through all the difficulties
which lie ahead.

but deliver us from evil

We acknowledge our continual need for God's grace and protection:
without him we can do nothing.

The Hail Mary

Hail Mary, full of grace,
the Lord is with thee.
Blessed art thou among women
and blessed is the fruit of thy womb, Jesus.

Holy Mary, Mother of God:
pray for us, sinners,
now at at the hour of our death. Amen.

Ave Maria, gratia plena;
Dominus tecum;
benedicta tu in mulieribus,
et benedictus fructus ventris tui, Jesus.
Sancta Maria, Mater Dei,
ora pro nobis peccatoribus
nunc et in hora mortis nostrae. Amen.

We never pray on our own, but always as part of the church.
Our prayer is shared by the faithful of all times and places, and
especially by the saints, in whom the life of Christ was most fully
their own, those in whom the spirit of prayer was most truly the
driving force in their lives. Together with them we form a single
family of God's children, and support each other by prayer.
We pray for many people, but we always draw strength and hope
from the fact that the saints pray for us.

Mary is the first of all the saints, the one in whom the Son of God
himself became man. She bore him in her womb and taught him
his first lessons in human life and love. As Mother of God she is also
our mother, the one in whom we admire the fullness of the life of
grace in which we grow through friendship with her Son.

The first part of the prayer repeats the angel Gabriel's greeting to
Mary bringing the news of Jesus' conception in her womb. Mary
is the greatest of all the saints because of her special part in the
redemption of the world by Christ. When we pray to Mary we are

celebrating the fact that God filled her with the grace she needed to be able to say 'yes' to God's invitation and to undertake the responsibility which would follow from that. She freely accepted all that this would involve, even though she could not yet begin to understand what it meant. We also have to try to give birth to Christ in our own lives day by day, which makes Mary's faith and obedient love of God a good example for us too. We pray to her so that she may pray for us. She knows what it takes!.

The second part of the prayer speaks about 'now' and 'the hour of our death'. The present moment and our final end are the only things that ultimately matter for our relationship with God. Whatever happens or has happened, at every moment of our lives 'now' is the only time that really exists, the real point of time where we can discover God, the heart of all reality; that means we can always turn to God and receive his mercy and strength; this is what we need and what Mary the mother of divine grace is praying for on our behalf. We put ourselves in her hands to commend us to God.

The Glory Be

**Glory be to the Father, and to the Son, and to the Holy Spirit:
as it was in the beginning, is now and ever shall be,
world without end.   Amen.**

Gloria Patri, et Filio,
et Spiritui Sancto:
sicut erat in principio,
et nunc, et semper,
et in saecula saeculorum.   Amen.

This simple prayer teaches us to worship God as the Trinity. It is the
simplest Christian prayer of adoration, Praising God simply for being
God, however little we can understand of the fullness of God's life
this side of the grave. As Father, Son and Holy Spirit, God shares a
full and perfect life from all eternity. The wonderful thing is that the
energy of that life lies at the origin of the creation of the universe as
well as of our own lives; and as human beings we are called by God
to take a share in it because we are his children.

It reminds us that all the glory of God's creation is only a reflection
of the true glory we find in the worship of the Father, through the
Son by the power of the Holy Spirit. But we also need to remember
that God shows his glory not only in beauty and power; we discover
it also in the suffering of his Son on the cross, for this is how the
pain and evil of this world is transformed into new life through the
Holy Spirit which makes all things new.

The Apostles' Creed

I believe in God, the Father almighty,
creator of heaven and earth;
and in Jesus Christ, his only Son, our Lord,
who was conceived by the Holy Spirit,
born of the Virgin Mary,
suffered under Pontius Pilate,
was crucified, died and was buried.
He descended into hell.
On the third day he rose again from the dead;
he ascended into heaven,
and is seated at the right hand of the almighty Father.
From there he shall come to judge the living and the dead.
I believe in the Holy Spirit,
the holy catholic Church,
the Communion of Saints,
the forgiveness of sins,
the resurrection of the body,
and life everlasting. Amen.

To pray is to make a statement of faith, and the creeds of the Church
have been used as prayers of worship as well as declarations of belief.
The Apostles' Creed is a statement of Christian faith which originated
in the early Roman Church. The modern Profession of Faith used at
Baptism and Confirmation is based on it. It gives a summary of our
knowledge of God: his existence as Father, Son and Holy Spirit; the
dependence of everything on him; the love and mercy which God
shows continually towards us, through the life and death of Jesus
Christ, as well as the way in which we share in his resurrection
through the Holy Spirit and the life of the Church. It celebrates the
community of faith we share with all Christians living and departed,
both sinners and saints. More than a statement of faith, it expresses
our hope of life with God forever.

The Nicene Creed

We believe in one God,
the Father, the Almighty,
maker of heaven and earth,
of all that is, seen and unseen.
We believe in one Lord, Jesus Christ,
the only Son of God,
eternally begotten of the Father,
God from God, Light from Light,
true God from true God,
begotten, not made, of one Being with the Father.
Through him all things were made.
For us men and for our salvation
he came down from heaven:
by the power of the Holy Spirit
he became incarnate from the Virgin Mary, and was made man.
For our sake he was crucified under Pontius Pilate;
he suffered death and was buried.
On the third day he rose again
in accordance with the Scriptures;
he ascended into heaven
and is seated at the right hand of the Father.
He will come again in glory to judge the living and the dead,
and his kingdom will have no end.
We believe in the Holy Spirit, the Lord, the giver of life,
who proceeds from the Father and the Son.
With the Father and the Son he is worshipped and glorified.
He has spoken through the Prophets.
We believe in one holy catholic and apostolic Church.
We acknowledge one baptism for the forgiveness of sins.
We look for the resurrection of the dead,
and the life of the world to come. Amen.

At Mass it is customary to make the Profession of Faith on Sundays
and major holy days using the Nicene Creed. The name comes from

the fact that in its original form it was accepted by the first ecumenical council of the Church held at Nicea in 325 as a basic statement of its trinitarian faith and in particular of the divinity of Christ. Subsequent reflection on the divinity of the Holy Spirit and on the nature of the incarnation of the Son of God led to changes, especially at the subsequent councils of Constantinople in 381 and Chalcedon in 451. Its character as a celebration of our common faith has led to its inclusion at Mass, but it also deserves to be prayed and reflected on in private.

11: Prayers for Every Day

Christians have always prayed early in the morning and evening as a way of dedicating their whole day to God. Morning and evening are the natural times for attending to our friendship with God; they are times when our minds are less caught up in the business of life, and when we can remind ourselves what the ultimate meaning of that life is. The first Christians also prayed at the beginning, the middle and the end of the working day to keep the concerns and difficulties of ordinary life in perspective, to remind themselves of the point of it all. In fact the Apostle Paul urges us to pray at all times, and at least if we can make special times for prayer at the beginning and end of our day, we will find it easier to build up a habit of spontaneous prayer throughout the day.

In the Morning

In the morning we remember God as the origin and goal of our life; he has given us a new day and it is a time for looking ahead. We dedicate ourselves and everything that lies ahead of us to him and ask for his help in what we have to do. Do not try to rush things. Start slowly and gently, putting yourself in the presence of God.

A simple pattern to use to start with might be:

(Sign of the Cross)
In the name of the Father and of the Son and of the Holy Spirit. Amen.

Our Father ...
Glory be ...

Then spend some time thanking God and worshipping him.

Adoration or praise leads into other acts of prayer, such as acts of faith, hope and love.

Think about the day ahead and pray for the tasks you have to complete.

Pray for the people you will meet and any special needs.

You might think about the difficulties and temptations which occur every day and the sins you want to avoid.

If you have had a chance to hear the news, you could pray more generally for other people.

Dedicate yourself to God's service; entrust yourself to him and to the prayers of the saints, especially the Virgin Mary.

Adoration and thanksgiving

As we wake up, we can think gratefully of the wonder of life,
something sacred which we have been given to live; we need time
to ponder on the meaning of life, something which we can only
explore one day at a time, constantly returning to God, the source
of life and of our hopes for fulfilment. To explore the meaning of
life is to begin a journey in search of God.

These prayers are dominated by the image of light: we cannot
live without it. The light of the sun is an image of Jesus Christ who
rises in our hearts and minds, and gives warmth as well as light.
The created world reflects the glory of a God who remains invisible,
at the heart of creation. The sight of the things God has made should
turn us inwards to look for the source of their beauty and energy.

O God, creator of light, at the rising of your sun this morning, let the
greatest of all lights, your love, rise like the sun within our hearts.

Armenian Church

O Lord, when I awake and day begins,
waken me to your presence,
waken me to your indwelling,
waken me to inward sight of you,
and speech with you and strength from you,
that all my earthly walk may waken into joy
and my spirit leap up to you all day all ways.

E. Milner-White

Eternal Father of my soul,
let my first thought today be of you,
let my first impulse be to worship you,
let my first speech be your name,
let my first action be to kneel before you in prayer.

John Baillie

O Lord, our heavenly Father, almighty and everlasting God,
you have safely brought us to the beginning of this day;
defend us in the same with your mighty power,
and grant that this day we fall into no sin,
neither run into any kind of danger;
but that all our doings may be ordered by your governance,
to do always that which is righteous in your sight,
through Jesus Christ our Lord.

adapted by The Book of Common Prayer
from the monastic office of Prime

Prayer to the Holy Spirit

Real prayer is something which God pours out in our hearts through
the Holy Spirit (Romans 5.5). The Spirit is the source of the life we
share in Christ. Through the Holy Spirit we are born again in Jesus
Christ as children of God, and through him we cry out 'Abba, Father'
(Romans 8.15). Prayer is a work of love: we love because God loved
us first.

O heavenly King, O Comforter, O Spirit of truth,
you are present everywhere and fill all things;
you are a treasury of blessings, the giver of life;
come and abide in us.
Cleanse us from all impurity and save our souls,
O good one.

St John Chrysostom

Almighty God, unto whom all hearts are open,
all desires known, and from whom no secrets are hid;
cleanse the thoughts of our hearts
by the inspiration of your Holy Spirit,
that we may perfectly love you
and worthily magnify your holy name;
through Christ our Lord.

The Book of Common Prayer

Acts of faith, hope and love

Adoration

O my God, I believe in you, strengthen my faith.
All my hopes rest in you, let me not be disappointed.
I love you with all my heart,
teach me to love you daily more and more.

Thanksgiving and contrition

O my God, how good you have been to me,
and how little I have done for you.
You have created me out of nothing,
redeemed me by the death of your Son,
and sanctified me by the grace of the Holy Spirit.
You have called me into your Church,
and given me the present day in which I may serve you.

Dedication and supplication

What return can I make to you for all you have done for me?
I will bless your holy name and serve you all the days of my life.
I will offer to you all the thoughts, words, actions and sufferings of this day,
and I beg you to give me your grace that I may not offend you this day,
but may faithfully serve you and do your holy will in all things.
Blessed be the holy and undivided Trinity now and for ever.

Prayers for the day ahead

Jesus wants us to ask his Father for everything we need. Think over the things which have to be done today, the problems which have to be faced, and any other concerns. Pray honestly for your own needs, and also for a sense of perspective. In the Sermon on the Mount Jesus also tells us not to worry about anything 'because your heavenly Father knows you need all these things'. He tells us only to 'strive rst for the Kingdom of God and his righteousness and all these things will be given you as well' (Matthew 6.32–34).

Go before us, Lord, in all our doings with your most gracious favour, and further us with your continual help; that in all our works begun, continued and ended in you, we may glorify your holy name, and finally by your mercy obtain everlasting life, through Jesus Christ our Lord.

The Book of Common Prayer

Light of the world, Lord Jesus Christ, shine on us so that we may walk steadfastly today in the path of life: give light to our minds and warmth to our hearts, so that your light may shine out in all we do and say.

Grant us grace, our Father, to do our work today as workmen who need not be ashamed. Give us the spirit of diligence and honest enquiry in our quest for truth, the spirit of charity in all our dealings with others, and the spirit of cheerfulness, courage and a quiet mind in facing all our tasks and responsibilities.

Reinhold Niebuhr

O Lord, you have taught us that to gain the whole world and to lose ourselves is great folly; give us the grace so to lose ourselves in service of those with whom we live and work that we may find ourselves renewed in the life of grace, and so to forget ourselves that you will remember us in your Kingdom.

Reinhold Niebuhr

O God, the source of peace and lover of concord,
in the knowledge of you consists eternal life,
in your service we find perfect freedom;
defend us, your humble servants, in all assaults of our enemies;
so that we who trust firmly in your defence
may not fear the power of any adversaries;
through the might of Jesus Christ our Lord.

The Book of Common Prayer

Open our hearts, O Lord, and enlighten us by the grace
        of your Holy Spirit,
that we may seek what is well-pleasing to your will;
and so order our lives according to your commandments,
that we may deserve to enter into your unending joy;
through Jesus Christ our Lord.

St Bede

Grant us, Lord, the spirit to think and do such things as be rightful,
that we, who cannot do anything that is good without you,
may be enabled by you to live according to your will;
through Jesus Christ our Lord.

Leonine Sacramentary

Lord, grant me to greet the coming day in peace.
Help me in all things to rely on your holy will.
In every hour of the day reveal your will to me.
Teach me to treat all that comes to me throughout the day with
        peace of soul,
and with firm conviction that your will governs everything.
In all my deeds and words guide my thoughts and feelings.
In unforeseen events let me not forget that all are sent by you.
Teach me to act firmly and wisely, without embittering and
        embarrassing others.
Give me the strength to bear the fatigue of the coming day
        with all that it shall bring.
Direct my will. Teach me to pray. Pray yourself in me.

Philaret of Moscow

Intercession

Pray for your home and family: mention people by name, give thanks for their love, and think of their special needs.

Think of the people you will meet today, and for the things which will bring you together.

Bless, O Lord, my parents, family and friends,
those who have done me good or evil,
and all for whom I ought to pray.
Let your fatherly hand always be over them;
let your Holy Spirit always be with them
and lead them in the knowledge and obedience of your Word,
that in the end they may obtain everlasting life.

Lord Jesus, I praise and thank you for my parents,
and my brothers and sisters, whom you have given me to cherish.
Surround them with your tender loving care;
teach us to love and serve one another and to look to you in all our needs.
I place them all in your care,
knowing that your love for them is greater than my own.
Keep us close to one another in this life,
and lead us at the last to our true and heavenly home.
Blessed be God for ever. Amen.

Pope John Sunday Missal

Prayer to the saints

We never pray on our own. We are part of a great family, the Communion of Saints, who inspire us with their lives and teaching, but, most important of all, pray for us.

Besides the Mother of God, the Mother of the Church and of all graces, St Joseph is the patron of work, and we have our patron saints who are specially close to us.

We should also remember the guardian angels who protect us. The prayers which follow could begin with the Hail Mary (see page 13). There are several other prayers to saints later on in the book.

Prayer to Mary
O Jesus, through the most pure heart of Mary,
I offer you all the prayers, thoughts, works and sufferings of this day
for all the intentions of your divine heart.

Prayer to St Joseph
Blessed Joseph, husband of Mary,
be with us this day.
You protected and cherished the Virgin:
loving the child Jesus as your Son,
you rescued him from danger of death.
Defend the Church, the household of God,
purchased by the blood of Christ.
Guardian of the holy family,
be with us in all our trials.
May your prayers obtain for us
the strength to flee from error
and wrestle with the powers of corruption
so that in this life we may grow in holiness
and in death rejoice in the crown of victory.

Prayer to one's patron saint
O heavenly patron, whose name I rejoice to bear,
pray for me always before the throne of God;
strengthen me in my faith; confirm me in virtue;
defend me in the fight, that being conqueror over the evil one
I may deserve to obtain everlasting glory.

Prayer to the angels

Lord God, creator of things visible and invisible, ever adored by the angels in heaven: support us through their loving protection and help us to find in their company the joy of doing your will and praising you in our lives; through Jesus Christ our Lord.

Lord, may your angels who supported Jesus in his times of trial always be near us to give us confidence in time of danger and uncertainty: for it is only by the strength of heaven that we can stand firm; through Jesus Christ our Lord.

Prayers of dedication

Finally commend yourself to God with these prayers of blessing.

May the strength of God guide me this day,
and may his power preserve me.
May the wisdom of God instruct me;
the eye of God watch over me;
the ear of God hear me;
the word of God give sweetness to my speech;
the hand of God defend me;
and may I follow the way of God.

Irish prayer

My hope is the Father,
my refuge is the Son,
my protection the Holy Spirit:
O Holy Trinity, glory to you.
All my hope I place in you, O Mother of God;
guide me under your protection.

Orthodox prayer

Christ be with me, Christ before me,
Christ be after me, Christ within me,
Christ beneath me, Christ above me,
Christ at my right hand, Christ at my left,
Christ in the fort, Christ in the chariot,
Christ in the ship,
Christ in the heart of every man who thinks of me,
Christ in the mouth of every man who speaks to me.
Christ in every eye that sees me.
Christ in every ear that hears me.

St Patrick

Set our hearts on fire with love for you, O Christ our God,
that in its flame we may love you
with all our heart, with all our mind, and with all our strength,
and our neighbours as ourselves,
so that, keeping your commandments, we may glorify you,
the giver of all good gifts.

Orthodox prayer

Guard for me my eyes, Jesus, son of Mary,
    lest seeing another's wealth make me covetous.
Guard for me my ears, lest they turn to slander,
    lest they listen constantly to folly in the sinful world.
Guard for me my heart, O Christ, in your love,
    lest I ponder the desire of any wrong.
Guard for me my hands,
    that they be not stretched out for quarrelling,
    that they may not after that reach out for unjust requests.
Guard for me my feet upon the gentle earth,
    lest hastening on pointless errands, they abandon rest.

Irish prayer

Assist us mercifully, O Lord, in these our supplications and prayers, and dispose the way of your servants towards the attainment of everlasting salvation; that among all the changes and chances of this mortal life, we may ever be defended by your most gracious and ready help; through Jesus Christ our Lord.

The Book of Common Prayer

Almighty Lord and everlasting God, we earnestly ask you to direct, sanctify and govern both our hearts and bodies in the ways of your laws and in the works of your commandments; that under your most mighty protection both here and ever we may be preserved in body and soul; through our Lord and Saviour, Jesus Christ.

The Book of Common Prayer

A child's prayer in the morning

Dear child divine,
Sweet brother mine,
Be with me all the day.
And when the light
Has turned to night
Be with me still I pray.
Wherever I be,
Come thou with me
And never go away.

During the Day

From early times Christians prayed regularly during the day for the renewing of God's help, especially as each day brought its difficulties and tiredness. A common theme in such prayer was the guidance of the Holy Spirit whose gifts help us to see things more clearly from God's point of view and to be courageous in living out the wisdom of the gospel. The Spirit enables us to live the new life of Christ and find our full freedom as human beings.

A special time of prayer is when we gather together to eat. Grace at table reminds us of how Jesus shared food with his followers. We remember our need both for spiritual and for physical food, as well as those who have little or nothing to eat.

Prayers for the Holy Spirit

Almighty God, the giver of all good things,
without whose help all labour is ineffectual,
without whose grace all wisdom is folly;
grant us the help of your Holy Spirit in all our undertakings,
so that all we do may be for your glory
and for the salvation of ourselves and others;
for the sake of Jesus Christ our Lord.

Samuel Johnson

Take not your Holy Spirit from me, O Lord,
and let me not allow evil thoughts to have dominion in my mind.
Let me not linger in ignorance and doubt,
but enlighten me and support me;
for the sake of Jesus Christ.

Samuel Johnson

O Holy Spirit, giver of light and life,
impart to us thoughts better than our own thoughts,
and prayers better than our own prayers,
and powers better than our own powers,
that we may spend and be spent
in the ways of love and goodness,
after the perfect image of our Lord and Saviour, Jesus Christ.

Eric Milner-White and G.W. Briggs

O come, Holy Spirit, inflame my heart, set it on fire with love.
Burn away my self-centredness so that I can live unselfishly.
Breathe your life-giving breath into my soul
so that I can live freely and joyously,
unrestricted by self-consciousness,
and may be ready to go wherever you may send me.
Come like a gentle breeze and give me your still peace
so that I may be quiet and know the wonder of your presence,
and help diffuse it in the world.
Never let me shut you out;
never let me try to limit you to my capacity;
act freely in me and through me; never leave me,
O Lord and giver of life.

Michael Hollings and Etta Gullick

Prayers for the working day

O God, the protector of all who trust in you,
without whom nothing is strong and nothing is holy,
increase and multiply your mercy upon us,
that with you as our ruler and guide
we may pass through the things of this world,
and gain that life that has no end;
for the sake of Jesus Christ our Lord.

The Book of Common Prayer

Father of all that is good, you have entrusted the world to mankind: help
us to delight in it and find in it a sign of your power and glory; may our
work not disfigure the beauty of what you have made, but in everything
give greater glory to you; through Jesus Christ our Lord.

Father of all mankind, you gave your only Son so that all who believe in
him may be saved: help us to live out our faith in all we do; help us to
meet everyone with whom we work as our brothers and sisters and
through our words and deeds build up the human family in peace and
happiness; through Jesus Christ our Lord.

Teach us, gracious Lord, to begin our works in a spirit of reverence for
you, to continue them in obedience, to finish them in love, and then to
wait patiently in hope, and with cheerful confidence look up to you,
whose promises are faithful and whose rewards are infinite; through
Jesus Christ our Lord.

George Hicks

Prayers in the middle of the day

Blessed Lord, by your life at Nazareth you made holy the ordinary work
of the day, and by your teaching revealed your compassion for those who
labour and are overburdened: grant that in the midst of our work we
may find rest and peace in your presence and joy in knowing that we are
serving you, who are our refuge and strength, and our exceeding great
reward.

O Christ, you are continually worshipped in heaven and on earth;
you are patience, compassion and mercy;
you love the righteous, you have mercy on sinners,
and you call us all to salvation, promising us the fullness of the life
   to come.
Receive our prayer in the middle of this day,
and make our life conform to your will;
sanctify our souls and bodies, order our thoughts,
and give us victory in all trials and sadness;
protect us and bless us,
so that we may come to the unity of faith and the knowledge of
   your glory,
for you live and reign with the Father and the Holy Spirit,
God for ever and ever.

based on Taizé Community prayer

Prayers at table

The first two of the following prayers are the traditional prayers used
at table.

For use before eating
Bless us, O Lord, and these your gifts which we are about to receive from
your bounty, through Jesus Christ our Lord.

For use after eating
We give you thanks, almighty God, for these and for all your blessings,
who live and reign for ever and ever.

Bless, Lord, this food you give us.
We thank you for those who have prepared it
and ask that this time will be one of fellowship and good cheer.
Help us not to forget those who are hungry, or in need;
make us eager to share what we receive with others
and to use the energy you give us in these gifts
not only to think but to work for peace and justice for all.

Bless, O Lord, this food and ourselves to your service,
through Jesus Christ our Lord.

In the Evening

In the evening we return to God in thanksgiving and praise for all his kindness through the day.

A simple pattern to use to start with might be:

(Sign of the Cross)
In the name of the Father and of the Son and of the Holy Spirit.
Amen.

Our Father ...
Glory be ...

Think over the day past and thank him for the good things of the day.

Be sorry for the bad things done, the good which you failed to do, and forgive those who have caused you hurt.

Pray for other people, especially those whose needs you have been made aware of during the day.

Commend yourself and those dear to you to God's protection during the night.

Opening up

It is a help to begin a time of evening prayer by gently gathering oneself together. Especially after a busy day we need to collect our thoughts and bring our minds and hearts back to the presence of God. It is often a help to do this in a place which is reasonably quiet and where we can ourselves quieten down. It is not easy even to sit still, and we need to learn to relax in a way which helps us to be attentive to God rather than just to wind down (and drift off to sleep!)

Think of the way a musician relaxes before starting a performance. All his powers need to be gathered together and find their centre in himself; then he can play with all his heart and mind. To do this when we pray we should find a good way of sitting or kneeling upright but without any stiffness, the weight evenly distributed on both sides of our body from the shoulders to the feet, with our head resting easily on the neck. Think in terms of balance. We also need to focus our minds, and begin to turn inwards again towards our centre, where the spirit lives in our hearts. We may find it best to close our eyes at least to begin with, but that is not always the best way to keep awake! Slowly and patiently we should try to turn our thoughts away from all that has happened, or all we have got to worry about for tomorrow, and as simply as we can try to keep turning our mind towards God. We will find all kinds of memories and feelings emerge. Whether they are positive or negative we should try to let go of them. Once we find our spiritual feet they can become the starting points of our prayer.

Hail gladdening Light, of his pure glory poured
Who is the immortal Father, heavenly, blest,
Holiest of Holies, Jesus Christ our Lord!
Now we are come to the sun's hour of rest,
The lights of evening round us shine,
We hymn the Father, Son and Holy Spirit divine.
Worthy are you at all times to be sung
With undefiled tongue,
Son of our God, giver of life, alone:
Therefore in all the world your glories, Lord, we own.

Orthodox hymn

Holy Spirit, I thank you for the quiet moments of this busy day
when you spoke to me of your abiding love.
Teach me now as I lay down to rest
how to listen to you in the silence of my heart.
Teach me how to listen to your still small voice
which gives meaning and direction to my life.

Michael Buckley

Eternal Light, shine into our hearts,
eternal Goodness, deliver us from evil,
eternal Power, be our support,
eternal Wisdom, scatter the darkness of our ignorance,
eternal Pity, have mercy upon us;
that with all our heart and mind and soul and strength
we may seek your face
and be brought by your infinite mercy to your holy presence;
through Jesus Christ our Lord.

Alcuin

Come, my Light, and illumine my darkness.
Come, my Life, and revive me from death.
Come, my Physician, and heal my wounds.
Come, Flame of divine love, and burn up the thorns of my sins,
kindling my heart with the flame of divine love.
Come, my King, sit upon the throne of my heart and reign there.
For you alone are my King and my Lord.

St Dimitrii of Rostov

Thanksgiving

Christians have always linked evening prayer with thanksgiving for
the death of Jesus, who died in the afternoon. The sun sinks below
the horizon, but its light does not fail even though we no longer see
it. Just as the rising sun is a sign of new life, so the setting of the sun
is a time to thank God for all Jesus has done for us, loving us to the
end, and giving his life for us.

Thanks be to you, my Lord Jesus Christ,
for all the benefits and blessings which you have won for me,
for all the pains and insults which you have borne for me,
O most merciful Redeemer, friend and brother;
may I know you more clearly,
love you more dearly,
and follow you more nearly,
day by day.

St Richard of Chichester

O God, I thank you for life and being,
and for all the blessings of the past day;
for the love I have received and given,
for all the kindnesses I have received from others,
for your grace going before me and following after me.
Above all I thank you for him
through whom I know your love and receive your grace,
even Jesus Christ, my Lord and Saviour.

George Appleton

Forgiveness

In the evening, Jesus healed those brought to him who were sick
(Mark 1.32–34); he died to save us from our sins and from the
power of evil over our lives. He also knows our weaknesses and how
easy it is to fail to do what we know is right. After he rose from the
dead, his first gift to his disciples was forgiveness of their sins; his
second the gift of reconciliation and peace. He teaches us that God
is like a father who is always waiting for us, however far away from
him we stray. As soon as we turn towards him, he sees us and runs
to meet us, and brings us back home (Luke 15.20–24).

Lord God, our loving Father,
you know all my sins and failures,
my weaknesses and temptations.
I come to you with deep sorrow in my heart
for the wrong I have done and for the good I have failed to do.
Forgive me, accept me, and strengthen me,
now and always.

David Konstant

I pray for all those whom I have in any way grieved, vexed, oppressed or scandalized, by word or deed, knowingly or unknowingly; that you may forgive all our sins and offences against each other.

Take away, O Lord, from our hearts all suspiciousness, indignation, anger and contention, and whatever is calculated to wound charity or to lessen love of others.

Have mercy on me, O Lord; have mercy on all who seek your mercy; give grace to the needy; make us so to live that we may be found worthy to enjoy the fulfilment of your grace and attain to eternal life.

Thomas à Kempis

O Lord our God, forgive the sins I have this day committed, in word, deed or thought; forgive me for you are gracious and you love all men and women. Grant me peaceful and undisturbed sleep, send your guardian angel to protect and guard me from every evil, for you are the guardian of our souls and bodies and we give you glory, to the Father, the Son and Holy Spirit, now and for ever.

Russian Orthodox prayer

O Lord my God, thank you
for bringing this day to a close;
Thank you for giving me rest in body and soul.
Your hand has been over me
and has guarded and preserved me.
Forgive my lack of faith
and any wrong that I have done today,
and help me to forgive all who have wronged me.
Let me sleep in peace under your protection,
and keep me from all the temptations of darkness.
Into your hands I commend my loved ones
and all who dwell in this house;
I commend to you my body and soul.
O God, your holy name be praised. Amen.

Dietrich Bonhoeffer

Intercession

As we think over the day past, we remember those with whom we have spent it; we pray for their needs as we thank God for their gifts and everything we have been able to share with them. We also think of the needs of the world. We think of people who have asked us to pray for them, and others who might have done if they had had courage, or only known we would. We should especially think of people who are lonely and in despair – who have no one to pray for them. The following prayers can be used as a point of departure to pray from our own experience.

Bless, O Lord, my parents, family and friends,
those who have done me good or evil,
and all for whom I ought to pray.
Bless all who remember me in their prayers,
those who need mine,
and especially those who have no one to pray for them.
Comfort the poor, the afflicted,
all prisoners and travellers,
the sick and the dying.
Have pity on the souls of the faithful departed,
and grant to them and to all who seek you
a place of refreshment, light and peace

Lord, I thank you for all you have done for me today;
help me to see you more clearly in my life.
Remember all those I love;
teach me to be more generous towards them.
Stay close to those who have been with me today;
comfort those whom I have harmed;
forgive those who have hurt me;
bless those who have encouraged me.
May the work I have done today, Lord,
give glory to you,
and be of service to my neighbour.

Into your hands, our Lord and Father, we commend this night
our souls and bodies,
our parents and homes,
friends and servants,
our neighbours and relatives,
our benefactors and departed brothers and sisters,
all folk rightly believing,
and all who need your pity and protection:
shed the light of your grace upon us,
and grant us never to be separated from you,
O Lord and Trinity, God everlasting.

Edmund Rich

Almighty Father, who covers the earth in your divine mercy with the
curtain of darkness so that all who are weary may rest, grant us all to
rest in you this night. Let your grace comfort and support all who are
to spend it in sorrow, in loneliness, suffering or in fear.

We commend ourselves into your hands, together with all who are dear
to us. Strengthen and confirm your faithful people; stir up the careless,
relieve the sick, give peace to the dying, that your holy name may be
glorified in Jesus Christ, your Son, our Lord.

H. Stobart

Watch, dear Lord, with those who wake and weep tonight, and give your
angels charge over those who sleep. Tend the sick, O Lord, give rest to
the weary, bless the dying, soothe the suffering, shield those who rejoice,
and all for your love's sake.

St Augustine

Prayers for the night

Night is a time when one can feel lonely, vulnerable or exposed to fear. It is a time when the powers of 'spiritual darkness' come into their own. But by his death and burial, Jesus is close to us however black the night seems. The angels who kept him safe during the temptations in the desert also keep us safe in the hand of God. In spite of the darkness, we look forward to the beauty of the light of his Kingdom which shall never fail. Full of hope in God we prepare for sleep looking forward to the joy of the peace which the world cannot give.

Grant, O Lord God,
that we may cleave to you without parting,
worship you without wearying,
faithfully seek you,
happily find you,
for ever possess you, the only God,
who are blessed for ever, world without end.

St Anselm

Be present, O merciful God, and protect us through the silent hours of this night, that we who are wearied by the changes and chances of this fleeting world may repose upon your eternal changelessness; through Christ our Lord.

Leonine Sacramentary

O God from whom all holy desires, all good counsels and all just works do proceed: give unto your servants that peace which the world cannot give; that our hearts may be set to obey your commandments, and also that being defended by you from the fear of our enemies we may pass our time in rest and quietness; through the merits of Jesus Christ our Saviour.

The Book of Common Prayer

Lighten our darkness we beseech you, O Lord, and by your great mercy defend us from all perils and dangers of this night, for the love of your only Son, our Saviour Jesus Christ.

The Book of Common Prayer

Lord, support us all the day long, till the shadows lengthen and the evening comes, and the busy world is hushed, and the fever of life is over, and our work is done. Then in your mercy grant us a safe lodging and a holy rest, and peace at the last.

John Henry Newman

God be in my head, and in my understanding,
God be in mine eyes, and in my looking,
God be in my mouth, and in my speaking,
God be in my heart, and in my thinking,
God be at my end, and at my departing.

Book of Hours

A child's prayer at night

Matthew, Mark, Luke and John,
bless the bed that I lie on.
Before I lay me down to sleep
I give my soul to Christ to keep.
Four corners to my bed,
four angels there aspread,
two to foot and two to head
and four to carry me when I'm dead.
If I go by sea or land,
the Lord has made me by his right hand;
if any danger come to me,
sweet Jesus Christ, deliver me.
He's the branch and I'm the flower,
pray God send me a happy hour;
and if I die before I wake,
I pray that Christ my soul will take.

During a sleepless night

Abba, Father, the world is so quiet. Everyone is asleep except me. I worry about so many things. Now I worry that I will not have slept when it is time to get up. Help me to relax: to put aside disturbing thoughts and think instead of your closeness to me. In these moments of quiet I ask for your Spirit, the spirit who brings peace and tranquillity, to enfold me in his love, removing all fear and anxiety, and instilling his calmness into the very centre of my being.

Anthony Bullen

Prayers taken from Compline

In monastic communities, Compline is the last time of prayer together before going to bed and its prayers can be used by anybody. The following prayers are a selection.

May the Lord grant us a quiet night's rest and a perfect end.

The Confiteor
I confess to almighty God, to blessed Mary, ever virgin, to blessed Michael the archangel, to blessed John the Baptist, to the holy apostles Peter and Paul, and to all the saints, that I have sinned exceedingly in thought, word and deed, through my fault, through my own fault, through my own most grievous fault. Therefore I beseech blessed Mary, ever virgin, blessed Michael the archangel, blessed John the Baptist, the holy apostles Peter and Paul, and all the saints to pray for me to the Lord our God.

The Song of Simeon
Antiphon: Save us, O Lord, while we are awake; guard us while we sleep; that we may keep watch with Christ and rest with him in peace.

Master, now you are dismissing your servant in peace,
    according to your word;
for my eyes have seen your salvation,
    which you have prepared in the presence of all peoples,

a light for revelation to the Gentiles
   and for glory to your people Israel.

You are in the midst of us and we are called by your name: do not desert us, O Lord our God.

Jeremiah 14.9

Guard us, O Lord, as the apple of your eye;
hide us in the shadow of your wings.

Psalm 16(17).8

I will lie down in peace and take my rest:
for it is you, Lord, only that make me dwell in safety.
Into your hands, O Lord, I commend my spirit;
you have redeemed me, O Lord God of truth.

Responsory adapted
from Psalm 30(31).5

Visit, O Lord, this house and family, and drive far from it all the snares of the enemy: may your holy angels dwell here to keep us in peace, and let your blessing be always upon us; through Christ our Lord.

Commendation

Night is a time also to remember that in God's good time we are going to sleep in death. This thought should help us see everything in its proper perspective; and that ought not to be one of despair, but rather of hope and longing for the fullness of life which cannot be contained in the space of a single life, let alone of a single day. We ought also to remember the departed, especially those whom we have known and for whom we should pray that God will bring them to the sight of his glory, but we should pray for all the dead who may have no one to remember them. Prayers for the dead can be found in a separate section (see pages 126–130).

Lord Jesus, you have prepared a place for my soul in your Father's house; prepare my soul for that place; prepare it with holiness; prepare it with desire; and even while it lives on earth, may it dwell in heaven with you, beholding the beauty of your countenance and the glory of all the saints, now and for evermore.

Joseph Hall, Bishop of Norwich

Into your hands, O Lord, I commend my spirit;
Lord Jesus, receive my soul.
Holy Mary, be a mother to me.
May our blessed Lady, St Joseph, and all the saints, pray for us to our Lord, that we may be preserved this night from all evil.

O my good angel, whom God, by his divine mercy, has appointed to be my guardian, enlighten and protect me, direct and govern me this night.

Jesus, Mary and Joseph, I give you my heart and my soul.
Jesus, Mary and Joseph, assist me in my last agony.
Jesus, Mary and Joseph, may I breathe forth my soul in peace with you.

May the souls of the faithful departed, through the mercy of God, rest in peace. Amen.

Prayers for Young People

Prayers for a school

Father, we thank you for your blessing on this school, and for the love and labour of all who have made it a house of faith and of fruitful study. Grant that we in our turn may follow their example, and may so learn truth as to bear its light along all our ways, and so learn Christ as ever to be found in him.

King's College, Cambridge

O Lord our Saviour, you have warned us that you will require much of those to whom much is given; grant that we, whose lot is cast in so goodly a heritage, may strive together the more abundantly by prayer, by fasting and by works of mercy, and by every other appointed means, to extend to others what we so richly enjoy; and, as we have entered into the labours of others, may we labour so that in their turn others may enter into ours, to the fulfilment of your holy will, and our everlasting salvation.

St Augustine

Prayers for study

Grant, Lord, to all students
to love and know that which is worth knowing,
to praise that which pleases you most,
to value that which is most precious to you,
and to dislike whatsoever is evil in your eyes.

Thomas à Kempis

Eternal Light, the Sun of Righteousness, which never sets but always rises in our minds to give light, food, and gladness to all; we pray that you will shine on us in your mercy and shed the radiance of your holy light on the dullness of our understanding, and the dark mists of our sins and errors, by the merits of our Lord Jesus Christ, the Saviour of all mankind.

after Erasmus

Almighty God, in whose hands are all our human powers, grant that we may not waste the life you have given us on useless trifles; but enable us by your Holy Spirit to shun sloth and negligence, so that every day we may perform the tasks you have given us, and obtain in everything we do such success as will give most glory to you; for the sake of Jesus Christ.

Samuel Johnson

Let your blessing, Lord, rest upon our work this day.
Teach us to seek after truth and enable us to attain it;
but grant that, as we increase in the knowledge of earthly things,
we may grow in the knowledge of you;
for to know you is eternal life and happiness.

Thomas Arnold

Prayers for sport

Thank you, Lord, for the pleasure of sport, for the fun and excitement of playing, as well as for the enjoyment of watching. Help us always to keep our play honest and fair, good-natured and friendly. So may the world of sport glorify your name.

Mary Batchelor

Thank you for fitness and strength,
for the enjoyment of using it well.
Give me a sense of discipline to train my body properly,
and also the wisdom to know how to use your gifts properly.
Help me, whether I win or lose, to play fairly,
and to support others in my team.
When I win, keep me from boasting;
if I lose, keep me from making excuses.
Help me always to live so that I will have a healthy body
    and a healthy mind.

William Barclay

Lord God, my body as well as my soul is yours:
help me to use it as I should.
Help me to play with all my strength this afternoon,
and be thankful for the strength you have given me.
Help me also to be strong in mind,
not to shrink from the effort of winning,
and to remember that I can only do so as part of a team.
Give me courage that does not give way to arrogance, vanity, jealousy,
    bitterness or revenge.
Bless all of us who will be playing, and bless those who will watch.
May we all enjoy the game (and win!).

after Hubert van Zeller

Choir prayer

Lord, we pray that what we sing with our lips we may believe in our hearts,
and what we believe in our hearts we may show forth in our lives;
through Jesus Christ our Lord.

Prayers before serving Mass

Help us, Lord, to serve you with all our hearts and minds. As we stand
at your altar help us to be truly thankful for all you have done for us and
to offer you our service out of love in return for the love you show us;
through Jesus Christ your Son.

Lord Jesus Christ, King of eternal glory, I desire to come before you and
to receive the sacrament of your Body and Blood for the honour and glory
of your Holy Name, and for the good of my own soul. I desire it because
it is your desire and you have asked us to do this in remembrance of you.
I desire to come before you so that I may be one with you in the joy
which you share with your heavenly Father from all time, so that through
the Holy Spirit I may dwell in you and you in me and that nothing in life
or death may ever separate me from you.

Prayers after serving Mass

May your holy Body and Blood, sweetest Jesus, be to me sweetness of soul, salvation and holiness at all times, joy and peace in every tribulation, light and strength in every word and work, and my last protection in death.

St Thomas Aquinas

Lord Jesus Christ, may the love this Mass celebrates inspire all I shall do today; may your Holy Spirit guide me and may the heavenly food I have received help me to grow strong in your grace so that I may follow your path today. You are the Way, the Truth and the Life.

Prayers before an examination

O God, we start exams tomorrow. I have studied hard, but I am sure I haven't learned enough and I cannot always remember what I've learned. Help me to keep calm and not be worried, so I'll remember what I've learned and do my best. Then if I fail, I need not be ashamed; and if I pass, please help me not to boast but give my thanks to you for helping me to use the gifts which you have given. Thank you, God.

Nancy Martin

Help me, Lord, to keep my mind fixed on truth. Help me to concentrate on what I have learned and not to worry about anything else. You, who know all things, prompt my memory with the light of understanding that I may make good use of what I have been taught, and not let my knowledge go to waste. Thank you for my ability such as it is: help me to use it to the full and to remember that all your gifts of mind, body and spirit are for your glory and for the service of others.

A Downside pupil

Prayers at the start of term

I pray to you, almighty God, that during this term I may fight the good fight with the strength of our Lord Jesus Christ. Help me to do my best in work and in sport, and to be a good friend and companion to all those around me. Give me courage and help me never to give up on what I know to be right and good.

A Downside pupil

Almighty God, give light to our understanding that this term we may enjoy the fruits of our efforts, in work and in all we do, which we offer to your Son Jesus Christ in thanksgiving for the gift of our life.

A Downside pupil

Prayers at the end of term

Dear God, we thank you for all you have given us this term, the lessons we have learned, and for what we have achieved outside class (in sport or anything else). We are sorry for the wrong we have done. Thank you for all our friends and those with whom we have spent this term, and for our teachers from whom we have learned so much. We pray we will enjoy the holiday and come back ready to continue the good work and to praise you; through Jesus Christ our Lord.

A Downside pupil

O God of life and love, you are the true rest of the soul; we ask you to bless the holidays as a time of rest. Keep us from all harm and evil; draw us closer to you. Give light to our eyes that we may see you in the beauty of creation and find you in all our enjoyment. Grant that, strengthened in body and refreshed in soul by the life-giving energy of your Holy Spirit, we may serve you faithfully in the life to which you have called us; through Jesus Christ our Lord.

A Downside pupil

O God our Father, you alone satisfy the desire of every living thing, and give us strength for your service and rest for the renewal of our strength. Bless our labour and our rest, the serious times as well as our laughter, our sorrow as well as our joy. May all our life give you glory, and may you bless us as we go on our ways rejoicing in your gifts to us. May we go in your peace through Jesus Christ our Lord.

after George Lyttleton

Prayers for getting on with others

Lord Jesus, teach us how to be humble. Teach us how to live like you, respecting others however lowly, poor and unattractive they are. Teach us to complete our tasks as you did, in unhurried quietness of mind, not thinking we deserve something more exciting. Teach us to see how unworthy we are of all the gifts that you have given us, and not to regard them as ours by right. Help us to see how small we are in comparison with you, and in realising this forget our self-importance, and serve you and everyone in true humbleness of heart.

Etta Gullick

God of love, you have given us a new commandment, that we should love one another; we are unworthy of your love and wander away from you, but we pray that you will give us in all the time of our life on earth a mind forgetful of past ill will, a pure conscience, and a heart to love others even as you have loved us; through Jesus Christ our Lord.

Coptic prayer

God our Father, direct our ways and make us to increase and abound in love to one another and to all: that we may be established in purity of heart and in holiness before you at the coming of our Lord Jesus Christ and all the saints; through the same Jesus Christ our Lord.

adapted from 1 Thessalonians 3.11–13

Lord Jesus, you have taught us that we can only be forgiven as we ourselves forgive: help us to bear continually in mind our own shortcomings and our many failings. If we remember the injuries we suffer and never deserved, help us to remember the kindnesses we received and never earned, and the punishments we did deserve and never suffered. Help us to be thankful for your unfailing mercies and those of other people; for the sake of the glory of your Name.

Eric Milner-White and G.W. Briggs

Give us, Lord, a humble spirit that never takes your mercy for granted, but which keeps us mindful of all we have been forgiven. Make us tender and compassionate towards those who fall into temptation, mindful of our own weakness now and in the future. Make us watchful and sober-minded, looking ever to you for grace to stand upright and to persevere to the end.

Dean Vaughan

Dear God, help me to be human. Help me to be able to appreciate and bring out the best in everyone around me. You have created us, so that we are able to appreciate consciously all the gifts that you have given us. Lord, help me to appreciate all that you have given me. Help me to be truly human.

Teenager's prayer from Harare

Heavenly Father, in your wisdom you have made your children in your image and likeness; not in a single mould but in many, each reflecting in his own way something of your own glory: take away from us the pride of heart which strives to impress our image on others and give us the desire to see in them only the reflection of you, through Jesus Christ our Lord.

Eric Milner-White and G.W. Briggs

Give us a sense of humour, Lord, and also things to laugh about.
Give us the grace to take a joke against ourselves,
and to see the funny side of the things we do.
Save us from annoyance, bad temper, resentfulness against our friends.
Help us to laugh even in the face of trouble.
Fill our minds with the love of Jesus; for his name's sake.

A. G. Bullivant

God grant me the serenity to accept the things I cannot change,
courage to change the things I can,
and wisdom to know the difference.

Reinhold Niebuhr

O God, you have bound us together in this bundle of life:
give us grace to understand how our lives depend upon the courage,
the industry, the honesty and the integrity of others;
that we may be mindful of their needs, grateful for their faithfulness,
and faithful in our responsibilities to them.

Reinhold Niebuhr

O Lord, we know that we very often worry about the things that may
never happen.
Help us to live one day at a time,
and to live it for you, for your name's sake.

Beryl Bye

From the cowardice that dares not face new truth,
From the laziness that is contented with half truth,
from the arrogance that thinks it knows all truth,
Good Lord, deliver me.

Kenyan prayer

Almighty God, have mercy on all who bear me evil will and would do me
harm, and by whatever tender, merciful means you can in your infinite
wisdom best devise, amend and redress their faults and mine, and,
through the passion of our sweet Saviour Jesus Christ, make us all saved
souls in heaven together where we may ever live and love together with
you and your blessed saints, O glorious Trinity.

St Thomas More

Prayers for the future

God has created me to do him some definite service;
he has committed some work to me which he has not committed to
another. I have my mission – I may never know it in this life,
but I shall know it in the next.

I have a part in this great work; I am a link in a chain, a bond of
connection between persons. He has not created me for nothing. I shall
do good, I shall do his work; I shall be an angel of peace, a preacher of
truth in my own place, even while not intending it, if I do but keep his
commandments and serve him in my calling.

Therefore I will trust in him.
Whatever I am, wherever I am, I can never be thrown away.
If I am in sickness, my sickness can serve him;
in perplexity my perplexity may serve him.
He does nothing in vain. He knows what he is about.
I do not ask to see; I do not ask to know;
I ask simply to be used.

John Henry Newman

Stay with me, and then I shall begin to shine as you shine: so to shine as
to be a light to others. The light, O Jesus, will be all from you. None of it
will be mine. It will be you who shine through me upon others. Let me
praise you, in the way you love best, by shining on everyone around me.
Give light to them as well as to me, light them with me, through me.
Teach me to show your praise, your truth, your will. Make me preach
you without preaching; not by words but by my example and by the
catching force, the sympathetic influence, of what I do – by my visible
resemblance to your saints, and the evident fullness of the love which
my heart bears for you.

John Henry Newman

We are candles that only have meaning if we are burning, for only
then do we serve our purpose of being light. Free us from the cowardly
prudence that makes us avoid sacrifice and look only for security.
Losing one's life should not be accompanied by pompous or dramatic
gestures. Life is to be given simply, without fanfare, like a waterfall,
like a mother nursing her child, like the humble sweat of the sower
of seed. Train us, Lord, and send us out to do the impossible, because
behind the impossible is your grace and your presence; we cannot fall
into the abyss. The future is an enigma; our journey leads us on, giving
ourselves because you are waiting there in the night, in a thousand
human eyes brimming over with tears.

Luis Espinal

Prayers for vocations

Prayers for vocations to the priesthood
Lord Jesus Christ, shepherd of souls,
who called the apostles to be fishers of men,
raise up new apostles in your holy Church.
Teach them that to serve you is to reign:
to possess you is to possess all things.
Kindle in the hearts of your children the fire of zeal for souls.
Make them eager to spread your Kingdom upon earth.
Grant them courage to follow you,
who are the Way, the Truth and the Life.

Almighty God, give us priests:
to establish the honour of your holy name;
to offer the holy sacrifice of the Mass;
to give us Jesus in Holy Communion;
to proclaim the faith of Jesus;
to baptize and teach your people;
to tend your sheep;
to seek the lost;
to give pardon to the penitent sinner;
to bless our homes;
to pray for the afflicted;
to comfort the sorrowful;
to strengthen us in our last hour;
to commend our souls to your merciful love.
Almighty God, give us priests.

Holy Father, you gave us Christ as the shepherd of our souls;
may your people never fail for want of priests who care for them with his
great love.

God our Father, your will is that the whole world be saved and come
to the knowledge of the truth. Send workers into your harvest that the
gospel may be preached to every creature, and your people, gathered
together by the word of life and strengthened by the power of the
sacraments, may advance in the way of salvation and love.

Pope John Sunday Missal

Prayer for vocations to the religious life
Father, you inspire and bring to fulfilment every good intention.
Guide your people in the way of salvation and watch over those who
have left everything to give themselves entirely to you. By following
Christ and renouncing worldly power and profit, may they serve you
and your people faithfully in the spirit of poverty and humility.

Pope John Sunday Missal

Prayer for vocations to the monastic life
It is in the silence of our hearts, O Lord,
that your voice calls us gently to turn from self-will
and surrender to you in our monastic vocation.
We thank you for that hidden gift
and pray that many others
may hear your call to monastic life.
May your loving grace give us strength
to persevere in St Benedict's way of peace
and to witness faithfully
to the truth and love of your Kingdom.
We ask through Jesus Christ our Lord.

St Benedict's Prayer Book

Grant, Lord, that those whom you call
to enter the priesthood or religious life
may have the generosity to answer your call,
so that those who need your help may always find it.
We ask through Jesus Christ our Lord.

St Benedict's Prayer Book

Prayers for General Use
mainly of saints and famous people

Prayers of adoration and praise by St Francis of Assisi

Praised be my Lord God for all his creatures,
especially for our brother the sun, who brings us the day and the light;
fair is he and shines with a very great splendour; O Lord he shows
you to us.

Praised be my Lord for our sister the moon, and for the stars which he
has set clear and lovely in the heaven.

Praised be my Lord for our brother the wind, and for the air and clouds,
calms and all weather by which you uphold the life in all creatures.

Praised be my Lord for our sister the water, who is very serviceable to us
and humble and precious and clean.

Praised be my Lord for our brother fire, through whom you give us light
in the darkness; and he is bright and pleasant and mighty and strong.

Praised be my Lord for our mother the earth, who sustains us and keeps
us and brings forth fruits, and flowers of many colours, and grass.

Praise and bless the Lord and give thanks to him and serve him with great
humility.

You are holy, Lord, the only God,
and your deeds are wonderful.
You are strong; you are great;
You are the most high, the almighty;
You, holy Father, are King of heaven and earth.
You are Three and One, Lord God, all good.
You are good, all good, supreme good,
Lord God, living and true.
You are love, and wisdom;
You are humility, endurance and peace;
You are joy and gladness;
You are justice and moderation;
You are all our riches, and you alone suffice for us.
You are beauty;
You are gentleness.
You are our protector, our guardian and defender.
You are our haven and our hope.
You are our faith, our great consolation.
You are our eternal life,
Great and wonderful Lord, God almighty, merciful Saviour.

St Patrick's Breastplate

I bind unto myself today
the strong name of the Trinity,
by invocation of the same,
the Three in One and One in Three.

I bind unto myself today
The power of God to hold and lead,
His eye to watch, his might to stay,
His ear to hearken to my need.
The wisdom of my God to teach,
His hand to guide, his shield to ward;
The word of God to give me speech,
His heavenly host to be my guard.

Christ be with me, Christ within me,
Christ behind me, Christ before me,
Christ beside me, Christ to win me,
Christ to comfort and restore me.
Christ beneath me, Christ above me,
Christ in quiet, Christ in danger,
Christ in hearts of all that love me,
Christ in mouth of friend and stranger.

I bind unto myself today
the strong name of the Trinity,
by invocation of the same,
the Three in One and One in Three.
Of whom all nature hath creation;
Eternal Father, Spirit, Word:
Praise to the Lord of my salvation,
Salvation is of Christ the Lord. Amen.

Prayer of thanksgiving

Almighty God, the Father of all mercies, we, your unworthy servants, give you humble and hearty thanks for all your goodness and loving-kindness to us and to all creatures.

We bless you for our creation, our preservation, and for all the blessings of this life; but above all for your inestimable love in the redemption of the world by our Lord, Jesus Christ, for the means of grace and for the hope of glory.

And we beg you to give us a fitting sense of all your mercies so that our hearts may be pure in thanksgiving, and that we may show forth your praise, not only with our lips but in our lives, by giving up ourselves to your service, and by walking before you in holiness and righteousness all our days; through Jesus Christ our Lord, to whom with you and the Holy Spirit be all honour and glory, world without end.

The Book of Common Prayer

Prayers for one's own needs – growth in faith and dedication

Many of the prayers in this section are about light and growth in understanding. This is not because we are becoming more and more expert in the knowledge of God, but so that we may learn how to live faithfully in the thick of everyday life. They are prayers to help us listen to our conscience and to have the heart to live courageously and generously for other people's good rather than only for ourselves. These prayers are arranged in approximately historical order.

O God, from whom to be turned is to fall,
to whom to be turned is to rise,
and in whom to stand is to abide for ever:
grant us in all our duties your help,
in all our perplexities your guidance,
in all our dangers your protection,
in all our sorrows your peace,
in everything your grace and blessing,
through Jesus Christ our Lord.

St Augustine

Eternal God, who are the light of the minds that know you,
the joy of the hearts that love you,
and the strength of the wills that serve you;
grant us so to know you, that we may truly love you,
and so to love you that we may fully serve you,
whom to serve is perfect freedom,
in Jesus Christ our Lord.

St Augustine

Here I am:
before you, Father, in righteousness and humility,
with you, my brother, in faith and courage,
in you, Spirit, in stillness:
Grant unto your servant
towards my God a heart of flame,
towards my neighbour a heart of love,
towards myself a heart of steel.

St Augustine

O gracious and holy Father,
give us wisdom to know you,
intelligence to understand you,
diligence to seek you,
patience to wait for you,
eyes to behold you,
a heart to meditate upon you,
and life to proclaim you;
through the power of the Spirit of Jesus Christ our Lord.

attributed to St Benedict

Lord God almighty, I pray you by your great mercy
and by the token of the holy cross,
guide me to your will, to my soul's need, better than I can myself;
and shield me against my foes, seen and unseen;
and teach me to do your will,
>so that I may inwardly love you before all things
>with a clean mind and a clean body.
For you are my maker and my redeemer,
my help, my comfort, my trust and my hope.
Praise and glory be to you, now and for ever, world without end.

King Alfred

Lord Jesus Christ, let me seek you by desiring you,
>and let me desire you by seeking you;
let me find you by loving you,
>and let me love you in finding you.
I confess Lord, with thanksgiving,
that you have made me in your image,
so that I can remember you, think of you, and love you;
but that image is so worn and blotted out by my faults,
and darkened by the smoke of sin,
that it cannot do that for which it was made
unless you renew and refashion it.
Lord, I am not trying to make my way to your height,
for my understanding is in no way equal to that,
but I do desire to understand a little of your truth
which my heart already believes and loves.
I do not seek to understand so that I can believe,
but I believe so that I may understand;
and what is more, I believe that unless I believe I shall not understand.

St Anselm

Lord, make me an instrument of your peace;
    where there is hatred let me sow love,
    where there is injury let me sow pardon,
    where there is doubt let me sow faith,
    where there is despair let me give hope,
    where there is darkness let me give light,
    where there is sadness let me give joy.
O divine master, grant that I may
    not try to be comforted but to comfort,
    not try to be understood but to understand,
    not try to be loved but to love.
For it is in giving that we receive,
    it is forgiving that we are forgiven,
    and it is dying that we are born to eternal life.

St Francis of Assisi

Give us, Lord, a steadfast heart which no unworthy affection can drag down-wards; an unconquered heart which no tribulation can wear out; an upright heart which no unworthy purpose can tempt aside.

Bestow upon us also, O Lord our God, understanding to know you, diligence to seek you, wisdom to find you and a faithfulness finally to embrace you; through Jesus Christ our Lord.

St Thomas Aquinas

Teach us, good Lord, to serve you as you deserve, to give and not to count the cost, to fight and not to heed the wounds, to toil and not to seek for rest, to labour and not to ask for any reward, save that of knowing that we do thy will; through Jesus Christ our Lord.

St Ignatius Loyola

Take, Lord, all my freedom, and receive my memory, my understanding and my whole will; whatever I have and possess you have given to me; to you, Lord, I restore it wholly, and to your will I utterly surrender it for your direction. Give me a love of you only and your grace, and I am rich enough, nor do I ask for anything besides.

St Ignatius Loyola

Lord Jesus Christ, you have made me and redeemed me and brought me to where I am upon my way; you know what you would do with me: do with me according to your will.

King Henry VI

Lord Jesus Christ, you are the Way, the Truth and the Life:
let us not stray from you who are the Way,
nor distrust your promises who are the Truth,
nor rest in anything but you who are the Life,
    for beyond you there is nothing to be desired,
      neither in heaven nor in earth.

Erasmus

Most merciful Saviour, to know you with the Father and the Holy Spirit
    is life everlasting:
increase our faith so that we never stray from your truth,
increase our obedience so that we never swerve from your commandments,
increase your grace in us,
    so that, alive with your life,
    we may fear nothing but you,
      for nothing is more powerful than you;
    love nothing but you,
      for nothing is more lovable than you;
    glory in nothing but you,
      for you are the glory of the saints;
    and finally desire nothing but you,
      for you are full and perfect happiness
      in the unity of the Father and the Holy Spirit
      for all eternity.

Erasmus

Father in heaven, you have given us a mind to know you,
a will to serve you, and a heart to love you.
Be with us today in all that we do,
so that your light may shine out in our lives;
through Christ our Lord.

St Thomas More

Glorious God, give me grace to amend my life, and to have an eye to my end without grudge of death; for to those who die in you, good Lord, death is the gate of a wealthy life.

And give me, good Lord, a humble, lowly, quiet, peaceable, patient, charitable, kind, tender, and pitiful mind; and with all my thoughts, words and deeds, to have a taste for your holy and blessed Spirit.

Give me, good Lord, a full faith, a firm hope and a fervent love, a love for you far stronger than my love for myself.

Give me, Lord, a longing to be with you, not for the sake of avoiding the troubles of this world, nor for the sake of the joys of heaven, but simply for love of you.

And show me, good Lord, your own love and favour which I can never deserve by my own love of you, except through your own great goodness.

These things, good Lord, that I pray for, give me the grace to labour for.

St Thomas More, before his execution

Almighty and everlasting God, give increase to your children's faith, hope and love, and so that we may obtain what you promise, help us to love what you command; through Jesus Christ our Lord.

The Book of Common Prayer

Almighty God, you alone can order the unruly wills and affections of sinful people: grant that we may love the things you command us and desire the things you promise, so that among the many and various changes of the world, our hearts may be surely fixed where true joys are to be found; through Jesus Christ our Lord.

The Book of Common Prayer

Grant us rest from all sinful deeds and thoughts, and to surrender ourselves wholly to you and keep our souls still before you like a still lake, so that the beams of your grace may be mirrored therein and kindle in our hearts the glow of faith and love and prayer. Through such stillness and hope, may we find strength and gladness in you, O God, now and for ever.

Joseph Embden

Lord, you know how busy I must be today.
If I forget you, do not forget me.

Jacob Astley
(before the battle of Edgehill)

Lord, make your way plain before me.
Let your glory be my end, your Word my rule,
and then, your will be done.

King Charles I

Perfect in us, O Lord, whatever is lacking in your gifts:
increase our faith;
establish our hope;
enkindle our love;
and make us fear nothing except to fear anything more than you,
our Father, our Saviour and our Lord.

Lancelot Andrewes

I hand over to your care, Lord,
my soul and body,
my mind and thoughts,
my prayers and hopes,
my health and work,
my life and death,
my parents and family,
my friends and neighbours,
my country and all people,
today and always.

Lancelot Andrewes

Lord Jesus, I give you
my hands to do your work,
my feet to go your way,
my eyes to see as you do,
my tongue to speak your words,
my mind that you may think in me,
my spirit that you may pray in me.
Above all, I give you my heart
    that you may love in me your Father and all mankind,
I give you my whole self
    that you may grow in me,
so that it is you, Lord Jesus,
who live and work and pray in me.

Lancelot Andrewes

O Lord, take full possession of my heart, raise there your throne and command there as you command in heaven. Being created by you, let me live to you. Being created for you, let me always act for your glory. Being redeemed by you, let me return to you what is yours, and let my spirit ever cling to you alone; for your name's sake.

John Wesley

O Lord, whose way is perfect, help us always to trust in your goodness: that walking with you in faith and following you in all simplicity, we may possess quiet and contented minds, and cast all our care on you, because you care for us; for the sake of Jesus Christ our Lord.

Christina Rossetti

O Lord, because we often sin and have to ask for pardon, help us to forgive as we would be forgiven, neither mentioning old offences committed against us, nor dwelling upon them in thought, but loving our neighbour as you love us; for your name's sake.

Christina Rossetti

Lift up our hearts, O Christ,
above the false shows of the things of this world,
above laziness and fear, above selfishness, envy and greed,
above custom and fashion,
up to the everlasting Truth that you are,
and which shines in the depth of our hearts;
so that we may live joyfully and freely
in the faith that you are our King and our Saviour,
our Example and our Judge;
and that as long as we are loyal to you,
all will be well with us in this world and in all worlds to come.

Charles Kingsley

Stir us up, O Lord, to offer you our bodies, souls and spirits
in all we love, in all we learn, in all we plan, and in all we do;
may we offer our labours, our pleasures and our sorrows to you,
so that you may work through them for the glory of your kingdom,
and so that we may live as people who are not our own, but bought
with your blood, fed with your body, people who belong to you
from the hour of our birth, now and for ever.

Charles Kingsley

Grant, O God, that we may wait patiently as servants standing before
    their Lord to know your will;
that we may welcome all truth, however it is expressed,
that we may bless every good deed, whoever is the doer of it,
that we may rise above all prejudice and party interest
to the contemplation of eternal Truth and Goodness
through the knowledge of Jesus Christ our Lord.

Charles Kingsley

Guide me, teach me, strengthen me, till I become such a person as you
would have me be: pure and gentle, truthful and high-minded, brave
and able, courteous and generous, dutiful and useful.

Charles Kingsley

Take from us, O God, all pride and vanity, all boasting and forwardness, and give us the true courage that shows itself by gentleness, the true wisdom that shows itself by simplicity, and the true power that shows itself by modesty.

Charles Kingsley

My Father, I abandon myself to you;
do with me as you will.
Whatever you may do with me, I thank you.
I am prepared for anything, I accept everything.
Provided your will is fulfilled in me and in all creatures,
I ask for nothing more, my God.
I place my soul in your hands.
I give it to you, my God,
with all the love of my heart
because I love you.
And for me it is a necessity of love, this gift of myself,
this placing of myself in your hands
without reserve
in boundless confidence
because you are my Father.

Charles de Foucauld

Thou who art over us,
Thou who art one of us,
Thou who art –
also within us,
may all see Thee – in me also,
may I prepare the way for Thee,
may I thank Thee for all that shall fall to my lot,
may I also not forget the needs of others,
Keep me in Thy love
as Thou wouldest that all should be kept in mine.
May everything in me be directed to Thy glory
and may I never despair.
For I am under Thy hand,
and in Thee is all power and goodness.
Give me a pure heart – that I may see Thee,
a humble heart – that I may hear Thee,
a heart of love – that I may serve Thee,
a heart of faith – that I may abide in Thee.

To love life and men as God loves them – for the sake of their infinite
possibilities,

    to wait like Him
    to judge like Him
    without passing judgement,
    to obey the order when it is given
    and never look back –
    then He can use you – then, *perhaps*, He will use you.
    And if he does not use you – what matter. In His hand,
every moment has its meaning, its greatness, its glory,
its peace, its co-inherence.

                    Dag Hammarskjöld

In times of doubt and uncertainty

Time and again we discover how little we really do understand, how easily we lose track of God. These are times when our faith is put to the test as Jesus' was in the Garden of Gethsemane and on the Cross. Our experience of life leaves us with many puzzles and sometimes forces us to ask very hard questions about the meaning of our life, and of life as such. It is not easy even to frame the questions because the problem seems to be that there is no one we can put them to, and we do not feel at all sure what sort of answer there is to them. In fact they are not the sort of questions that need answers so much as questions which need to be lived through: they are part of our experience of ourselves, our very existence brings them to the surface.

At these times then, it is important to be very honest about ourselves and the best prayer is perhaps the hardest – prayer from our own feelings, bringing them to the surface, and not shying away from the difficulty we have, but sharing our feelings with whoever, whatever. The fact that we do not see God, or feel him, can reveal more about our own need and poverty of spirit than about God, who is closer to us than we can ever think or imagine.

The following are prayers for faith, hope and love. They are uttered in the dark rather than the light; but like all real prayer they utter the most real of our needs – our need for God. And as we learn to live by faith, we can pray more trustingly in him, and less out of our own confusion.

Be patient to all that is unsolved in your heart . . .
Try to love the questions themselves . . .
Do not now seek the answers,
which cannot be given because you would not be able to live them.
And the point is to live everything.
Live the questions now.
Perhaps you will then gradually, without noticing it,
live along some distant day into the answers.

Rainer Maria Rilke

O my God, I believe in you, help my unbelief:

I believe in all you have revealed and teach through your Church because you are Truth itself and can neither deceive nor be deceived.

I hope in you for grace and for glory because of your promises, your mercy and your power.

I love you with my whole heart and above all things because you are so good, and for your sake I will love my neighbour as I love myself.

Grant that I may love you more and more in this life and in the next for all eternity.

Lord, give us grace to hold fast to you when all is weariness and fear, when sin abounds within and without, when I cannot do what I would, and when I do what I would not, when love is tested by doubt that my love is false or dead within the soul, when every act brings new confusion or new distress, when new opportunities bring new misunderstandings, and every thought an accusation. Lord, give us grace that we may know that in the darkness pressing round it is the mist that hides your face; that you are there and you know we still love you.

Gilbert Shaw

Lord, I believe in you; help my unbelief.
I love you, yet not with a perfect heart as I would;
I trust in you, yet not with my whole mind.
Accept my faith, my love, my longing to know and serve you,
    my trust in your power to keep me.
Kindle what is cold; make up what is lacking;
I wait for your blessing through Jesus Christ our Lord.

Malcolm Spencer

Lord, I want to love you, yet I'm not sure.
I want to trust you, yet I'm afraid of being taken in.
I know I need you, yet I'm ashamed of the need.
I want to pray, yet I'm afraid of being a hypocrite.
I need my independence, yet I fear to be alone
I want to belong, yet I must be myself.
Take me, Lord, yet leave me alone.
Lord, I believe; help my unbelief.
O Lord, if you are there, you do understand, don't you?
Give me what I need but leave me free to choose.
Help me to work it out my own way, but don't let me go.
Let me understand myself, but don't let me despair.
Come to me, O Lord; I want you there.
Lighten my darkness, but don't dazzle me.
Help me to see what I need to do and give me strength to do it.
O Lord, I believe; help my unbelief.

Brother Bernard SSF

Let nothing disturb you,
Nothing affright you;
All things are passing,
God never changes.
Patient endurance
Attains to all things;
Who God possesses
In nothing is wanting:
Alone God suffices.

Saint Teresa of Avila

My Lord God, I have no idea where I am going.
I do not see the road ahead of me.
I cannot know for certain where it will end.
Nor do I really know myself,
and the fact that I think I am following your will
does not mean that I am actually doing so.
But I believe that the desire to please you does in fact please you.
And I hope I have that desire in all that I am doing.
I hope that I will never do anything apart from that desire.
And I know that if I do this
you will lead me by the right road
though I may know nothing about it.
Therefore I will trust you always
    though I may seem to be lost and in the shadow of death.
I will not fear, for you are ever with me,
    and you will never leave me to face my perils alone.

                              Thomas Merton

Where are you, God?
I cannot feel anything except myself here,
Everything is just empty and cold.
I reach out and there is nothing to hold on to;
everything I have taken for granted about you seems to have gone.
I have lost my bearings and
sometimes I feel I am losing my mind.
Help me to find you even in this emptiness,
help me to find you as the space in which I live,
in whom I live and move and have my being,
even when it is a hard and painful mystery to me.
Open my heart and help me to grow even in this emptiness
so that I may understand you as you are,
not as I have supposed you to be.
Help me to know you, my God,
always greater than my thoughts,
always greater than my hopes,
ever-faithful, ever-living God.

Prayers of repentance and renewal

Lord God, there is no counting your mercy
and no limit to your goodness:
hear our prayer as we thank you for all you have given us;
enable us to examine our lives with the light of your spirit;
fill us with grace, mercy and peace,
so that we may live in truth and love
and grow in holiness;
through Jesus Christ, our Lord.

Monastic Ceremonial

Spirit of God, you speak to spirits created in your own likeness: penetrate
into the depths of our spirits, into the storehouse of memories,
remembered and forgotten, into the depths of being, the very springs
of personality; cleanse and forgive, making us whole and holy, that we
may become more truly like you and and live in the new being of Christ
our Lord.

George Appleton

Lord Jesus, you have taught us that love is the fulfilling of the law. Teach
us what love really is, how much it costs, how far it leads, how deep it
digs into our selfish selves. Then give us the courage and generosity to
accept what this means today and tomorrow and in the whole future
of our lives.

Michael Hollings

My God and Father, help me to pray as my first work, my unremitting
work, my highest, finest and dearest work; as the work I do for you and
by you and with you, for all your children and for the whole world.
Infuse it and influence it with your Holy Spirit, that it be not unwilling
nor unworthy nor in vain; that it be not occupied with my own concerns
nor dwell in the interests dear to myself; but seek your purposes, and
your glory alone, that it be holy and more holy to the Holiest, and ever
and all through your Son, my Saviour Jesus Christ.

Eric Milner-White

Prayers for other people

We beg you, Lord, to help and defend us.
Deliver the oppressed, pity those who count for little in the world;
raise the fallen, show yourself to the needy, heal the sick,
bring back those of your people who have gone astray,
feed the hungry, lift up the weak, set prisoners free.
May all nations come to know that you alone are God,
that Jesus Christ is your Child,
that we are your people, the sheep of your pasture.

St Clement of Rome

Lord, Jesus Christ, good shepherd of the sheep, who came to seek out
the lost and to gather them into your fold; have compassion on those
who have wandered away from you; feed those who are hungry, make
the weary lie down in green pastures, bind up the broken in heart and
strengthen the weak, so that we may rely on your care, be comforted by
your love and stand firm under your guidance to the end of our lives;
for the sake of your name.

Blessed Lord, you have commanded us to love one another: grant us,
who have not deserved the generosity of your kindness, the grace to
love everyone in you and for you. We implore your kindness on all, but
especially on the friends whom your love has given us. Love them, O
fountain of love, and grant them to love you with all their heart, that they
may will and speak and do those things only which are pleasing to you.

St Anselm

Almighty and eternal God, may your grace enkindle in all of us a love
for those people whom poverty and misery reduce to a condition of life
unworthy of human beings. Arouse in the hearts of those who call you
Father a hunger and thirst for justice and peace and for fraternal charity
in deeds and in truth. Grant, O Lord, peace in our days: peace to our
souls, peace to our families, peace to our country and peace among
nations.

Pope Pius XII

Lord, we pray for the power to be gentle;
the strength to be forgiving;
the patience to be understanding;
the endurance to accept the consequences of holding fast to what we
    believe to be right.
May we put our trust in the power of good to overcome evil and the
    power of love to overcome hatred. We pray for the vision to see and
    the faith to believe in a world emancipated from violence, a new
    world where fear shall no longer lead people to commit injustice,
    nor selfishness make them bring suffering to others.
Help us to devote our whole life and thought and energy to the task of
    making peace, praying always for the inspiration and the power to
    fulfil the destiny for which we and all mankind were created.

Week of Prayer for World Peace

Make us worthy, Lord, to serve our brothers and sisters throughout the
world who live and die in poverty and hunger. Give them through our
hands this day their daily bread, and by our understanding love, give
peace and joy.

Mother Teresa of Calcutta

Christ has no body now on earth but yours: no hands but yours: no feet
but yours. Yours are the eyes through which must look out Christ's
compassion on the world. Yours are the feet with which he is to go about
doing good. Yours are the hands with which he is to bless mankind now.

St Teresa of Avila

For the Pope
Almighty and eternal God, have mercy on your servant Pope _____
and direct him according to your mercy into the way of everlasting
salvation; that he may desire by your grace those things that are
pleasing to you and perform them with all his strength; through
Jesus Christ our Lord.

For the Church

Most glorious and most bountiful God, accept our praises and
thanksgivings for your holy catholic Church, the mother of us all who
bear the name of Christ, for the faith which it has handed on in safety to
our time, and the mercies by which it has enlarged and comforted the
hearts of mankind; for the virtues which it has established in the world,
and the holy lives by which it gives glory both to the world and to you;
to you be all honour, might, majesty and dominion, O Blessed Trinity,
now and for ever.

Memorials

O God of unchangeable power and eternal light, look favourably on your
whole Church, that wonderful and sacred mystery, and by the tranquil
operation of your perpetual providence, carry out the work of salvation:
that things which were cast down may be raised up, and that all things
may return to unity through him by whom all things were made, even
your Son Jesus Christ our Lord.

Gelasian Sacramentary

For world peace

Almighty God, from whom all thoughts of truth and peace proceed;
kindle, we pray, in all our hearts the true love of peace; and guide with
your pure and peaceable wisdom those who take counsel for the nations
of the earth, that in tranquillity your Kingdom may go forward, till the
earth is filled with the knowledge of your love; through Jesus Christ
our Lord.

Bishop Francis Paget

For the Queen

Almighty God, whose kingdom is everlasting and power infinite, bless
our country, and so rule the heart of your chosen servant Elizabeth
our Queen, that she, ever knowing whose servant she is, may above all
things seek your honour and glory; and that we, duly considering whose
authority she has, may faithfully serve, honour and humbly obey her,
in you and for you, according to your holy Word; through Jesus Christ
our Lord.

adapted from The Book of Common Prayer

For the government

Sovereign Master, you have given authority and kingship to those who rule and lead us on earth – so marvellous that power of yours our words cannot express it – so that seeing the glory and honour you have provided for them, we should be subject to their rule without resisting your will.

Grant them, Lord, the health, peace, concord and stability to use that sovereignty aright which you have bestowed on them.

For you, King of Heaven, are the one who gives mankind glory and honour and power over our world.

Lord, make their counsels conform to what is good and pleasing to you, that using the power you have given them with reverence, peacefully and gently, they may find favour with you.

St Clement of Rome

For benefactors

God our Father, you inspired the generosity of many benefactors, known and unknown, from the harvest of whose lives we are reaping today: make us also faithful to your kindness in our day, that we may sow a generous harvest which others shall reap hereafter.

Eric Milner-White and G.W. Briggs

Almighty God, your desire is for all to be saved and your mercy is without end, we beg you to show your loving kindness on your servant _____ and all our relatives, friends and benefactors who have passed from this world, that at the intercession of the Blessed Virgin Mary and all the saints you will grant them eternal happiness in your presence.

Roman rite

Pour out your love on our family and on all who give so much of themselves through their care for us. Help us to appreciate their gifts and their generosity in sharing them; help us to learn from them how to make our own your gift of life to us. May we learn how to be generous and to show our thanks in using our lives for others. May we be able to help others learn how much you love them through your Son, Jesus Christ our Lord.

A final prayer

Almighty God, you have given us grace at this time with one accord to make our common supplications unto you, and promise that when two or three are gathered together in your name you will grant their requests; fulfil now, Lord, the desires and petitions of your servants as may be most expedient for them, granting us in this world knowledge of your truth and in the world to come life everlasting.

St John Chrysostom

A Christian Week

Just as a day has a natural rhythm from dawn to nightfall which Christians have used to give shape to their daily prayer, in the Christian tradition the week has an underlying rhythm of its own which is played out in various times and seasons of the year. The weekly rhythm is special because, in the story of Genesis, God created the heavens and the earth in seven days. The week measures a God-given span for our work, which should include a chance to rest from our labours as God did on the seventh day, the Saturday or Sabbath, in order to enjoy the beauty of what he had made. Christians keep Sunday, the first day of the week, holy because it is the day on which the Lord rose from the dead, the start of the new creation. Sunday is the high point of the Christian week. To prepare for this celebration of the resurrection Christians remembered Jesus' celebration of the Last Supper and his Passion on the preceding Thursday and Friday. Saturday was devoted to the memory of Mary's part in our redemption by Jesus.

Prayers for Thursday

see *Prayers for Mass and Holy Communion* (pages 89 and following)

Prayers for Friday

Before midday
Lord Jesus, as you set out on the way of the Cross in obedience to your Father's will, help us to be faithful to the path you have marked out for us by your life and death and to find peace in the power of your Cross.

At midday
Lord Jesus, you gave your life for the salvation of all the world: help us to follow your example and stretch out our arms in mercy to all our brothers and sisters, and by your grace to serve them with a love like yours.

In the afternoon

Lord Jesus, as we look on the cross on which you died, help us to repent of all the wrong we do: and by our sorrow melt away all the hardness in our hearts so that we may strive with you to overcome the power of evil in the world.

Blessed Saviour, who at this hour hung on the cross stretching forth your loving hands to draw all things to yourself; grant that all mankind may look to you and be saved.

Lord, in answer to our prayer, give us patience in suffering hardships after the example of your Only-begotten Son Jesus Christ, who lives and reigns for ever and ever.

Roman rite

Prayers for Saturday

Bless us, Father of all creation, as we rest from our work: help us to share your delight in the world you have made and in the life you have given us. May your Spirit refresh us, renew our health and strength, and make us more eager to serve you in body and soul; through Jesus Christ our Lord.

Heavenly Father, as you filled Mary with grace and made her the mother of our Saviour, renew our faith, hope and love so that we may grow in his image and likeness and share with her in the joy of heaven; through the same Jesus Christ our Lord.

III: Prayers of Blessing

General prayers of blessing

The grace of our Lord Jesus Christ, and the love of God, and the fellowship of the Holy Spirit, be with us all evermore.

Bless all who worship you, almighty God, from the rising of the sun to its setting: from your goodness enrich us, by your love inspire us, by your spirit guide us, by your power protect us, in your mercy receive us, now and always.

Ancient Collect

May the Father of heaven grant us from the riches of his glory to be strengthened by the Spirit in our inmost hearts, so that Christ may dwell in our hearts through faith, and that, in him, we may be rooted and grounded in love and have the power to comprehend with all the saints the full measure of his love which surpasses knowledge, and be filled with all the fullness of God.

adapted from Ephesians 3.16–19

May God, the Lord, bless us and make us pure and holy in his sight. May the riches of his glory abound in us. May he instruct us with the word of truth, inform us with the gospel of salvation, and enrich us with his love; through Christ our Lord.

Gelasian Sacramentary

We commend ourselves to God's gracious mercy and protection. May the Lord bless us and keep us. May he make his face shine upon us and be gracious unto us. May he lift up the light of his countenance upon us, and give us peace, now and evermore.

Aaronic blessing

Prayers of blessing for the home

Bless this house, O Lord, and all who live in it as you were pleased
to bless the house of Abraham, Isaac and Jacob; may an angel of light
dwell within it so that we and all who live together here may receive
the abundant dew of your heavenly blessing and through your tender
mercy rejoice in peace and quiet; through Jesus Christ our Lord.

Gelasian Sacramentary

O God, make the door of this house wide enough to receive all who
need human love and fellowship, and a Father's care; and narrow
enough to shut out all envy, pride and hate. Make its threshold smooth
enough to be no stumbling block to children or to straying feet, but
rugged enough to turn back the tempter's power. Make it a gateway
to your eternal Kingdom.

Thomas Ken

Blessing with holy water

The words of Psalm 50(51) can be used with holy water, to bless anything. Water is a sign of the Holy Spirit, which cleanses and irrigates our hearts. It is a symbol of the waters of creation and of our new creation in Christ. Any of the verses of the psalm could be used, such as the following:

Have mercy on me, O God, according to your steadfast love;
according to your abundant mercy blot out my transgressions;
wash me thoroughly from my iniquity,
and cleanse me from my sin.

You desire truth in the inward being;
therefore teach me wisdom in my secret heart.
Purify me, and I shall be clean.
Wash me, and I shall be whiter than snow.

Create in me a clean heart, O God,
and put a new and steadfast spirit within me.
Do not cast me away from your presence,
and do not take your Holy Spirit from me.

Prayer to be used with holy water

Make the sign of the cross on yourself with holy water and sprinkle it over those to be blessed. The following prayer can be used:

This water reminds us of our baptism; let us ask God to keep us faithful to the Spirit he has given us.

Lord, in your mercy, give us living water always springing up as a fountain of salvation. Free us, body and soul, from every danger and admit us to your presence in purity of heart; through Jesus Christ our Lord.

Prayers before a journey

Almighty God, you show your mercy at all times to those who love you, and are close to all who serve you, direct the paths of your servants in your will, so that with you as their protector and guide, they may always walk in the paths of justice and of peace, through Jesus Christ our Lord.

Gelasian Sacramentary

Preserve from all danger, we beseech you, O Lord, all who travel by land, sea or air. Give them all the help they need on their way and grant that they may walk steadfastly in the paths of your commandments and attain the end of their faith, the salvation of their souls and the eternal dwelling place you provide for your children; through Jesus Christ our Lord.

after R. M. Benson

To your fatherly protection, O Lord, we commend ourselves and those about to travel. Bless, guide and defend us, that we may so pass through this world as finally to enjoy in your presence everlasting happiness; for Christ's sake.

Samuel Johnson

Almighty God, the clouds are your chariot and you walk on the wings of the wind, be a companion to all who are travelling by air, that you may guide them; support them and bring them safely to their destination. For you are the creator, sustainer and goal of all life; we ask this through Jesus Christ our Lord.

IV: Prayers for Mass, Holy Communion and Benediction

The Mass is the principal way in which we worship God, because at Mass we celebrate the sacrament of Our Lord's death and resurrection. We do what Jesus told us to do, taking and sharing his body and blood under the appearances of bread and wine 'in memory of me'. The central eucharistic prayer is a thanksgiving for what God has done through Jesus Christ who gave his life for the salvation of all people; we also offer ourselves to God as people who are part of his body, so that just as we have life through Jesus, so the world may live through us.

Prayers before Communion

It is one thing to get ourselves physically into a church, another to
gather our minds and hearts into the presence of God. Jesus taught
that the sacrifice which is pleasing to God is offered by a contrite
heart, that is, by people who know in their hearts how much God
has done for them. The worship of God is spiritual worship, although
as human beings we need the physical signs of the sacraments to
express what we are. Worship is a matter of the heart. So we should
begin our preparation for Mass not only by thanking God for what he
has done for us, but also by confessing what we have done, good or
bad, so that God can forgive our sins and we can offer him something
of ourselves.

The Mass is also a prayer we offer for the world and for ourselves.
Jesus himself prayed for his disciples before his passion and for all
people when he was on the cross. The first part of the Mass ends
with the Prayer of the Faithful on Sundays and normally a priest will
offer the Mass for a special 'intention', that is a special request which
he will be praying for during the Mass. You can also think over the
special needs you know about for which you can join with the priest
in offering the sacrifice of the Mass. It is a Christian privilege to share
in the intercession of Christ who is the High Priest of the new and
eternal covenant.

The other prayers in this section are to help us remember the
meaning of the Mass so that we can enter into it more fully, and
receive what God wants to give us.

Almighty God, unto whom all hearts are open, all desires known, and
from whom no secrets are hid; cleanse the thoughts of our hearts by
the inspiration of your Holy Spirit, that we may perfectly love you and
worthily magnify your holy name; through Christ our Lord.

The Book of Common Prayer

With all my heart I desire to celebrate this Mass and to receive the body
and blood of our Lord Jesus Christ
to the praise of our all-powerful God, and all his assembly in the glory
of heaven (*think here of the season of the Church's year or the mystery of faith being
commemorated at this Mass, of the saint whose feast is being celebrated, your own
patron saints*)
for my own good (*pray for your own needs*)
and for the good of his pilgrim Church on earth (*pray for the Pope and the
mission of the Church, for your own Church and those who work in it*)
for all who have asked me to pray for them (*especially . . .*)
and all who need my prayers (*think of any special needs in the world*).
May the almighty and merciful Lord grant us joy and peace, amendment
of life, room for true repentance, the grace and comfort of the
Holy Spirit and perseverance in good works.

Roman rite

O Sacrum Convivium

This is a well known antiphon of St Thomas Aquinas. It puts the
Mass in its proper place, between the death and resurrection of Jesus,
by which we are saved, and the final celebration of his victory over
sin and death in the Kingdom of Heaven. In the meantime we not
only look backwards in faith, but also forwards in hope, and receive
the pledge of God's love which is with us all the time, preparing us
for heaven.

O sacrum convivium in quo Christus sumitur:
recolitur memoria passionis eius:
mens impletur gratia:
et futurae gloriae nobis pignus datur.

At this sacred banquet in which Christ is received
the memory of his passion is renewed,
our minds are filled with grace
and the promise of future glory is given to us.

Prayers of St Thomas Aquinas and St Ambrose

These two prayers are very well-known prayers used to prepare for Mass. They are best used as private meditations on the meaning of the Mass. A number of images are used, each of which has its own value in explaining how the Mass is central to the life of the Church and to our own life in God's company. In the Mass, we receive God's forgiveness, but also his healing and strength; God washes us, feeds us, and teaches us.

Above all the prayers are a meditation on the real presence of our Lord in the sacrament: just as he had during his life on earth a human body, so we receive in the sacrament a share in his risen body. This makes us, in our separate human bodies, part of the one Body of Christ which exists in the Church which celebrates the sacraments of our faith until everything is fulfilled in the new creation.

Almighty and ever-living God, I approach the sacrament of your
only-begotten Son, our Lord Jesus Christ.
I come sick to the doctor of life,
unclean to the fountain of mercy,
blind to the radiance of eternal light,
and poor and needy to the Lord of heaven and earth.
Lord, in your great generosity,
heal my sickness, wash away my defilement, enlighten my blindness,
enrich my poverty, and clothe my nakedness.
May I receive the bread of angels, the King of kings and Lord of lords, with
humble reverence, with the purity and faith, the repentance and love,
and the determined purpose which will help bring me to salvation.
May I receive the sacrament of the Lord's body and blood, as well as its
reality and power. Merciful God, may I receive the body of your
only-begotten Son, our Lord Jesus Christ, born from the womb of the
Virgin Mary, and so be united to his mystical body and be counted
among his members.
Loving Father, as on my earthly pilgrimage I now receive your beloved Son
under the veil of a sacrament, may I one day see him face to face in
glory, who with you in the unity of the Holy Spirit lives and reigns for
ever and ever.

St Thomas Aquinas

Lord Jesus Christ, I approach your banquet table in fear and trembling, for I am a sinner and dare not rely on my own worth but only on your goodness and mercy. I am defiled by many sins in body and soul, and by my unguarded thoughts and words.

Gracious God of majesty and awe, I seek your protection, I look to you for healing. Poor troubled sinner that I am, I appeal to you, the fountain of mercy. I cannot bear your judgement, but I trust in your salvation.

Lord, I show my wounds to you and uncover my shame before you. I know my sins are many and great, and they fill me with fear, but I hope in your mercies, for they cannot be numbered.

Lord Jesus Christ, eternal King, God and man, crucified for mankind, look upon me with mercy and hear my prayer, for I trust in you. Have mercy upon me, full of sorrow and sin, for the depth of your compassion never ends.

Praise to you, saving sacrifice, offered on the wood of the Cross for me and for all mankind.

Praise to the noble and precious blood, flowing from the wounds of my crucified Lord Jesus Christ, and washing away the sins of the whole world.

Remember, Lord, your creature whom you have redeemed with your blood. I repent of my sins and long to put right what I have done. Merciful Father, take away all my offences and sins; purify me in body and soul, and make me worthy to taste the holy of holies.

May your body and blood which I intend to receive, although I am unworthy, be for me the remission for my sins, the washing away of my guilt, the end of my evil thoughts, and the rebirth of my better instincts. May it incite me to do the works which are pleasing to you and profitable to me in body and soul, and be a firm defence against the wiles of my enemies.

St Ambrose

The Prayer of Humble Access

The following prayer is adapted from a prayer taken from
the Anglican Communion Service. It is based on the Prayer of
St Ambrose.

We do not presume to come to this your Table, O merciful Lord,
trusting in our own righteousness, but in your many and great mercies.
We are not worthy even to gather up the crumbs under your Table.
But you are the same God whose property is always to have mercy: grant
us therefore, gracious Lord, so to eat the flesh of your dear Son Jesus
Christ, and to drink his blood, that our sinful bodies may be made clean
by his body, and our souls washed through his most precious blood,
and that we may evermore dwell in him and he in us.

The Book of Common Prayer

Other prayers of preparation

Lord Jesus Christ, to whom belongs all that is in heaven and earth,
I desire to consecrate myself wholly to you and be yours for evermore.
This day I offer myself to you in singleness of heart, to serve and obey
you always, and I offer you without ceasing a sacrifice of praise and
thanksgiving. Receive me, O my Saviour, in union with the holy oblation
of your precious blood which I offer to you this day, in the presence of
angels, that this sacrifice may avail unto my salvation and that of the
whole world.

Thomas à Kempis

Give me, good Lord, a full faith and fervent charity,
a love of you, good Lord,
incomparable above the love of myself;
and that I love nothing to your displeasure
but everything in order to you.

Take from me, good Lord, this lukewarm fashion, or rather, this cold
manner of meditation, and this dullness in praying to you.
Give me warmth, delight, and life in thinking about you.
And give me your grace to long for your holy sacraments
and specially to rejoice in the presence of your blessed body, my sweet
Saviour Jesus Christ, in the holy sacrament of the altar,
and duly to thank you for your graciousness in giving yourself to me.

St Thomas More

Holy Spirit, cleanse our minds and hearts so that we may celebrate with
joy the mysteries of our redemption in this holy Mass. Be near us as we
bring our gifts to the Father, in union with the Son, who as our supreme
high priest has gone through highest heaven there to make intercession
for us. Fill us with confidence in approaching the throne of grace
where, with the angels and saints, we shall render due homage through
Jesus Christ who with you and the Father lives and reigns, God, for ever
and ever.

Prayers after Communion

These prayers can be said either immediately after receiving Holy Communion, or after the Mass is over. Especially while you are waiting for Communion to finish or in the quiet prayer which follows, it is good to think about the generosity of Jesus' love on the Cross. The *Anima Christi* and the *Prayer before a Crucifix* are two traditional prayers used for this.

Anima Christi

Soul of Christ, be my sanctification,
Body of Christ, be my salvation,
Blood of Christ, fill my veins.
Water from the side of Christ, wash out my stains.
May Christ's Passion strengthen me,
O good Jesus, hear me.
In thy wounds I fain would hide,
Never to be parted from thy side.
Guard me when my foes assail me,
Call me when my life shall fail me.
Command me then to come to thee.
That I for all eternity
With thy saints may praise thee.

Pope John XXII
(translated by John Henry Newman)

Prayer before a Crucifix

My good and dear Jesus, I kneel before you, asking you most earnestly
to engrave upon my heart a deep and lively faith, hope and love, with
true repentance for my sins, and a firm resolve to make amends.

As I reflect on your five wounds and dwell upon them with deep
compassion and grief, I recall, good Jesus, the words the prophet
David spoke long ago concerning yourself:

> they have pierced my hands and my feet, they have counted all my bones.

Prayers of offering and dedication

The first three of these prayers are taken from the Anglican Service
Books, although the second has roots in the Roman Canon on which
The Book of Common Prayer based its prayers which followed
Communion.

Father of all, we give you thanks and praise, that when we were still far
off you met us in your Son and brought us home. Dying and living, he
declared your love, gave us grace, and opened the gate of glory. May we
who share Christ's body live his risen life; we who drink his cup bring life
to others; we whom the Spirit lights give light to the world. Keep us firm
in the hope you have set before us, so we and all your children shall be
free, and the whole earth live to praise your name; through Jesus Christ
our Lord. Amen.

Almighty God,
we thank you for feeding us
with the body and blood of your Son Jesus Christ.
Through him we offer you our souls and bodies
to be a living sacrifice.
Send us out in the power of your Spirit
to live and work to your praise and glory. Amen.

Remember, O Lord, what you have wrought in us, and not what we
deserve; and as you have called us to your service, make us worthy of our
calling; through Jesus Christ our Lord.

The Book of Common Prayer

You know better than I how much I love you, Lord. You know it and I know it not, for nothing is more hidden from me than the depths of my own heart. I desire to love you; I fear that I do not love you enough. I beg you to grant me the fullness of pure love. Behold my desire; you have given it to me. Behold what you have placed in your creature. O God, you love me enough to inspire me to love you for ever; do not look on my sins, but on your mercy and love.

François Fénélon

Set our hearts on fire with love to you, O Christ our God, that in that flame we may love you with all our heart, with all our mind, with all our soul, with all our strength, and our neighbours as ourselves; so that keeping your commandments, we may glorify you, the giver of all good gifts.

Orthodox prayer

O Jesus, receive my poor offering. Jesus, you have given yourself to me – now let me give myself to you: I give you my body that it may be chaste and pure. I give you my soul that it may be free from sin. I give you my heart that it may love you always. I give you every breath that I shall breathe and especially my last. I give you myself in life and in death that I may be yours for ever.

Lord Jesus Christ, take all my freedom,
my memory, my understanding and my will.
All that I have and cherish you have given me.
I surrender it all to be guided by your will.
Your grace and your love are wealth enough for me.
Give me these, Lord Jesus, and I ask for nothing more.

St Ignatius Loyola

Be light to my eyes, music to my ears, sweetness to my taste, and full contentment to my heart. Be my sunshine in the day, my food at table, my repose in the night, my clothing in my nakedness, my support in all necessities. Lord Jesus, I give you my body, my soul, all I have, my fame, my friends, my liberty and my life. Dispose of me and all that is mine as seems best to you and to the glory of your name.

John Cosin

We bless and praise you, Father, for you have accepted from our hands these simple gifts making them holy, a sign of your endless love for us and for all mankind. By our communion make us signs that we are your children. Grant that, as the bread which was broken on the altar was given to us as the food of life, we may give ourselves generously in all we do for the life of others. We thank you, Father, for we have received your Son. It is he who transforms us, makes us new, a living promise of your hope to all people. May we live as witnesses to your Son, who has come and who will come again, and so give you, your Son, and the Holy Spirit glory and praise, now and for ever.

Pope John Sunday Missal

Father, we are your chosen people.
May we live with compassion, kindness, humility and patience.
May we forgive each other as you forgive us.
May we live with the love which brings everyone together in
    perfect harmony.
May the peace of Christ reign in our hearts.
May the words we speak and the deeds we perform in your Son's name
    tell you of our thanks and praise.

Pope John Sunday Missal

Use me, my Saviour, for whatever purpose and in whatever way you may require. Here is my poor heart, an empty vessel; fill it with your grace. Here is my sinful, troubled soul; give it life and refresh it with your love. Take my heart for your dwelling place; my mouth to tell out the glory of your name; my love and all my powers for the growth of your people, and never let the steadfastness and confidence of my faith abate.

Dwight Moody

My Lord and my God – thank you for drawing me to yourself. Make me desire more deeply that knowledge which is eternal life. Lord, you have told us that the pure shall see God – the single-minded who do not try to serve two masters, who have no other gods but you. Keep my desire for you burning as brightly and steadily as a candle – a single, undivided focus of attention, a steady offering of my heart and will. Let my whole being be filled with your light, so that others may be drawn to you. Let my whole being be cleansed by the flame of your love from all that is contrary to your will for me, from all that keeps others from approaching you. Let my whole being be consumed in your service so that others may know your love – my Lord and my God.

Margaret Dewey

A Prayer of St Thomas Aquinas

As with the prayer of St Thomas to be used before Mass, this is a meditation which can best be used slowly on one's own.

I give you thanks,
Lord, holy Father, everlasting God.
In your great mercy,
and not because of my own merits,
you have fed me with the precious body and blood
of your Son, our Lord Jesus Christ.
I pray that this holy communion
may not bring me judgement and condemnation,
but forgiveness and salvation.
May it be my armour of faith
and shield of good purpose.
May it root out in me all vice and evil desires,
increase my love and patience,
humility and obedience,
and growth in the power to do good.
Make it a firm defence against the wiles
of my enemies, seen and unseen,
while restraining all evil impulses of flesh and spirit.
May it help me to cleave to you, the one true God,
and bring me a blessed death when you call.
I beseech you to bring me, a sinner,
to that glorious feast where,
with you and the Holy Spirit,
you are the true light of your holy ones,
their flawless blessedness,
everlasting joy,
and perfect happiness;
through Christ our Lord.

St Thomas Aquinas

The Universal Prayer (attributed to Pope Clement XI)

This prayer is traditionally included among prayers after Mass.
It can be used in whole or in part, and any of it can be adapted for
use at any time.

Lord, I believe in you: increase my faith.
I trust in you: strengthen my trust.
I love you: let me love you more and more.
I am sorry for my sins: deepen my sorrow.

I worship you as my first beginning,
I long for you as my last end,
I praise you as my constant helper,
and call upon you as my loving protector.

Guide me by your wisdom,
correct me with your justice,
comfort me with your mercy,
protect me with your power.

I offer you, Lord, my thoughts to be fixed on you;
my words to have you for their theme;
my actions to reflect my love for you;
my sufferings to be endured for your greater glory.

I want to do what you ask of me:
in the way you ask,
for as long as you ask,
because you ask it.

Lord, enlighten my understanding,
strengthen my will,
purify my heart,
and make me holy.

Help me to repent of my past sins
and to resist temptation in the future.
Help me to rise above my human weaknesses
and to grow stronger as a Christian.

Let me love you, my Lord and my God,
and see myself as I really am:
a pilgrim in this world,
a Christian called to respect and love
all whose lives I touch,
those in authority over me
or those under my authority,
my friends and my enemies.

Help me to conquer anger with gentleness,
greed by generosity,
apathy by fervour.
Help me to forget myself
and reach out towards others.

Make me prudent in planning,
courageous in taking risks.
Make me patient in suffering,
unassuming in prosperity.

Keep me, Lord, attentive in prayer,
temperate in food and drink,
diligent at my work,
firm in my good intentions.

Let my conscience be clear,
my conduct without fault,
my speech blameless,
my life well ordered.

Put me on guard against my human weaknesses.
Let me cherish your love for me,
keep your law
and come at last to your salvation.

Teach me to realize that this world is passing,
that my true future is the happiness of heaven,
that life on earth is short,
and the life to come eternal.

Help me to prepare for death
with a proper fear of judgement,
but with a greater trust in your goodness.
Lead me safely through death
to the endless joys of heaven.

From the Didache

This is part of one of the earliest Eucharistic prayers we have. It is a
beautiful witness to the hopes and prayers of Christians in the first
and second centuries for which they prayed at Mass.

We thank you, Father, for the holy vine of David, your servant, which you
have made known to us through your servant Jesus.
To you be glory for ever and ever!
We thank you Father for the life and knowledge you have made known to
us through your servant Jesus.
To you be glory for ever and ever!
In the same way that this bread which is now broken was scattered upon
the mountains and was gathered up again to become one, so may your
Church be gathered together from the ends of the earth into your
kingdom, for yours is the glory and the power through Jesus Christ for
ever and ever.
We thank you, Holy Father, for your Holy Name which you have made to
dwell in our hearts, and for the knowledge, faith and immortality which
you have made known to us through your servant Jesus.
To you be glory for ever and ever!

Prayers before the Blessed Sacrament

At the Last Supper Jesus took bread and wine and said 'This is my body' and 'This is my blood'; our Lord's words are repeated at every Mass in the eucharistic prayer, and because of this Catholics believe that the consecrated bread and wine embody Jesus' presence in a real and lasting way, as the Blessed Sacrament. This is reserved in churches in an honoured position in the tabernacle. It is a place where we can always go and find Jesus who lives at the heart of his Church. A visit to the Blessed Sacrament can be a good way to find a prayerful place in the midst of a hectic and distracting world. Any of the prayers given above can be used as well as those which follow. Because Jesus is so close to us, it is perhaps easy to feel we can pray just by being there looking at him and letting our thoughts turn towards him quite freely.

Adoration

O Sacrament most holy, O Sacrament divine,
All praise and all thanksgiving be every moment thine.

O heart of Jesus in the Blessed Sacrament, burning with love for us, inflame our hearts with love for thee.

May the heart of Jesus in the most Blessed Sacrament be praised, adored and loved, with grateful affection at every moment, in all the tabernacles of the world, even to the end of time.

Thanksgiving

My Jesus, I thank you with all my heart for your loving kindness to me. Blessed and praised every moment be the most holy and divine Sacrament.

Offering

My Jesus, in the most holy Sacrament you have given yourself to me: accept in return all the senses of my body and all the faculties of my soul. Give me light and grace: light to know your holy will and grace to do it.

Sorrow

My Jesus, too often have I offended you, and now, before you in the Blessed Sacrament, I ask the grace never to sin again.

Adoro te devote

Godhead here in hiding, whom I do adore
Masked by these bare shadows, shape and nothing more,
See, Lord, at thy service low lies here a heart
Lost, all lost in wonder at the God thou art.

Seeing, touching, tasting are in thee deceived;
How says trusty hearing? That shall be believed;
What God's Son has told me, take for truth I do;
Truth himself speaks truly or there's nothing true.

On the cross thy godhead made no sign to men;
Here thy very manhood steals from human ken:
Both are my confession, both are my belief,
And I pray the prayer of the dying thief.

I am not like Thomas, wounds I cannot see,
But can plainly call thee Lord and God as he:
This faith each day deeper be my holding of,
Daily make me harder hope and dearer love.

O thou our reminder of Christ crucified,
Living bread the life of us for whom he died.
Lend this life to me then: feed and feast my mind,
There be thou the sweetness man was meant to find.

Bring the tender tale true of the Pelican;
Bathe me, Jesu Lord, in what thy bosom ran –
Blood that but one drop of has the worth to win
All the world forgiveness of its world of sin.

Jesu whom I look at shrouded here below,
I beseech thee send me what I thirst for so,
Some day to gaze on thee face to face in light
And be blest for ever with thy glory's sight.

attributed to St Thomas Aquinas
(translated by Gerard Manley Hopkins)

Hymn of St Alphonsus

O bread of heaven, beneath this veil
thou dost my very God conceal:
my Jesus, dearest treasure, hail;
I love thee and adoring kneel;
each loving soul by thee is fed
with thine own self in form of bread.

O food of life, thou who dost give
the pledge of immortality;
I live; no, 'tis not I that live;
God gives me life, God lives in me:
he feeds my soul he guides my ways,
and every grief with joy repays.

O bond of love, that dost unite
the servant to his living Lord;
could I dare live and not requite
such love — then death were meet reward:
I cannot live unless to prove
some love for such unmeasured love.

Beloved Lord in heaven above,
there, Jesus, thou awaitest me;
to gaze on thee with changeless love,
yes, thus I hope, thus shall it be:
for how can he deny me heaven
who here on earth himself hath given?

Benediction of the Blessed Sacrament

The service of Benediction originated in the late Middle Age with the processions which were held on the feast of Corpus Christi, during the course of which the Blessed Sacrament was held up for veneration. In time such expositions became common throughout the year, as an opportunity to give thanks for the Mass and to meditate on Christ's abiding presence in the Church.

The association of Mary with prayer to the Blessed Sacrament is based on the fact that it is through her that Jesus became a human being, with the living body which was raised from the dead and is venerated in the sacrament he left us as his eternal memorial.

Benediction can be a beautiful service, a chance to surround our prayer with music and light which befits the worship of God, and to bring before him all the thoughts and intentions of our hearts. We ask for forgiveness for those times we have failed to do his will and thank him for the gifts he has given us. We praise him for his greatness and his goodness.

As the Blessed Sacrament is brought to the altar and placed in the monstrance, the following hymn is often sung.

O salutaris hostia,	O saving Victim, opening wide
Quae caeli pandis ostium;	The gate of heaven to man below;
Bella premunt hostilia,	Our foes press on from every side;
Da robur, fer auxilium.	Your aid supply, your strength bestow.
Uni Trinoque Domino	To your great name be endless praise,
Sit sempiterna gloria,	Immortal Godhead, one in three;
Qui vitam sine termino	O grant us endless length of days
Nobis donet in patria.	In our true native land with thee.
Amen	Amen

A short passage of Scripture, a meditation or a prayer may be read, which is followed by a short period of silent prayer before the Blessed Sacrament.

Then the following hymn is sung:

Tantum ergo Sacramentum	Therefore we before him bending
Veneremur cernui:	This great Sacrament revere;
Et antiquum documentum	Types and shadows have their ending
Novo cedat ritui:	For the newer rite is here;
Praestet fides supplementum	Faith, our outward sense befriending,
Sensuum defectui.	Makes the inward vision clear.
Genitori Genitoque	Glory let us give, and blessing
Laus et jubilatio	To the Father and the Son;
Salus, honor, virtus quoque	Honour, might, and praise addressing,
Sit et benedictio;	While eternal ages run;
Procedenti ab utroque;	Ever too his love confessing,
Compar sit laudatio.	Who, from both, with both is one.
Amen.	Amen.

V. *Panem de caelo praestitisti eis* (*Alleluia*)
You gave them bread from heaven (Alleluia)
R. *Omne delectamentum in se habentem.* (*Alleluia*)
Containing in itself all goodness. (Alleluia)

Oremus	Let us pray
Deus, qui nobis sub	O God, who in this wonderful
sacramento mirabili	sacrament have left us a memorial
passionis tuae memoriam	of your passion: grant, we
reliquisti: tribue,	beseech you, that by venerating the
quaesumus, ita nos	sacred mysteries of your body and
Corporis et Sanguinis tui	blood we may ever feel within us the
sacra mysteria venerari ut	fruit of your redemption: who live
redemptionis tuae fructum in	and reign for ever and ever.
nobis jugiter sentiamus: qui	
vivis et regnas in saecula	
saeculorum.	
Amen.	Amen.

The priest then blesses the congregation with the Blessed Sacrament. After this the Divine Praises are said.

The Divine Praises

Blessed be God.
Blessed be his holy name.
Blessed be Jesus Christ, true God and true man.
Blessed be the name of Jesus.
Blessed be his most Sacred Heart.
Blessed be his most Precious Blood.
Blessed be Jesus in the most holy Sacrament of the altar.
Blessed be the Holy Spirit, the Paraclete.
Blessed be the great Mother of God, Mary most holy.
Blessed be her holy and immaculate conception.
Blessed be her glorious assumption.
Blessed be the name of Mary, virgin and mother.
Blessed be St Joseph, her spouse most chaste.
Blessed be God in his angels and his saints.

While the priest is replacing the Blessed Sacrament in the tabernacle and leaving the Sanctuary, a eucharistic hymn or one of the following may be sung:

Adoremus in aeternum sanctissimum Sacramentum

Let us adore the most holy Sacrament for ever.

Laudate Dominum omnes gentes; laudate eum omnes populi. Quoniam confirmata est super nos misericordia ejus; et veritas Domini manet in aeternum.

O praise the Lord all you nations: acclaim him all you peoples. For his mercy is confirmed upon us and the truth of the Lord remains for ever.

Gloria Patri, et Filio, et Spiritui Sancto. Sicut erat in principio et nunc et semper, et in saecula saeculorum. Amen.

Glory be to the Father and to the Son And to the Holy Spirit. As it was in the beginning, is now, and ever shall be, world without end. Amen.

v : The Sacrament of Reconciliation

Preparation for Confession

Always begin by thanking God for his love in giving us life; he also promises us the fullness of life made new through Jesus; and he never stops loving us, but guides us all the time by the Holy Spirit. Even when we sin he is with us and our sense of right and wrong is a sign of God's presence in our hearts, however slow we are to think of him.

Make an act of faith in Jesus Christ who saves us from sin and death. He came not to condemn the world but to save it. He went out of his way to seek those who were lost and to give them a new sense of God's love. He believes in us more than we do ourselves and, with his eyes set on God, sees a future for us which only he can teach us to desire.

Jesus pours his Spirit into our hearts, the spirit of knowledge and understanding, of right judgement and courage, of reverence and wonder in God's presence. Ask the guidance of the Holy Spirit to help you see your sins truly but also to renew in your heart an appreciation of his love and patience with our weakness. Pray for courage to be honest in confessing them and for the grace of the sacrament to live more fully according to his will.

Heavenly Father, your love never ends.
I thank you for my life and being.
All that I am and all that I have is your loving gift to me.
I thank you for your generosity and patience with me,
for your constant mercy and loving kindness.

I thank you especially for the love you show me in Jesus Christ
who died for me so that I might share the fullness of life with him.
I am sorry that I have turned away from you.
I have rejected the guidance of the Holy Spirit, and allowed sin to enter
   my life.
I have turned away from Jesus whom I should love above everything else.

Renew your grace within me;
give me the light of your Holy Spirit to see what I have done wrong,
and the good I have failed to do.

Give me courage to return to you.
Receive me again into friendship with you,
and help me to be more generous in response to your love.

Deepen my commitment to the life of Christ I share within the Church,
   and help me to live for the good of all who belong to the human family.
Every day, help me to grow in your image to the full measure of life which
   you have prepared for me in your Son, Jesus Christ.

Examination of conscience

Our conscience is where we meet God. He gives light to our hearts so
that we can know right and wrong, good and bad. In preparing for
reconciliation with God as well as with ourselves and other people,
it is necessary that we return to our hearts and examine ourselves in
the light which we receive from God.

Our love can fall short of the love God shows us both because of
wrong we do and because of good we fail to do; we can sin in our
thoughts, in our words and in our deeds.

A simple way of thinking about this is to think about the place God
takes in our life; how we treat our family, friends, people with whom
we live and work in general; we should think how we have used our
own time and talents – selfishly or to help others.

There may be particular things on our conscience; they may be part of a wider pattern of behaviour or thinking about which we should pray.

It may help to use this litany, or one of the other lists which follow, as a meditation. Other people use a short passage of Scripture in prayer, letting it touch their conscience and illuminate perhaps only a single problem to bring to confession. We have to come clean about any serious sins, but otherwise it is not necessary or possible to mention everything. We should feel free to talk about the things which trouble us, always remembering that the important thing is to respond to the love God shows us in forgiving us anything which lies on our hearts.

Litany of repentance
Jesus asks us to love God with all our heart and soul and strength, and to love our neighbour as ourselves,
we should try to live as children whom the heavenly Father loves.
Let us turn to him in true repentance for our sins and failings
but with full confidence in him, for his great love endures for ever.

When we have been selfish, wanting our own way rather than to think of others,
when we have taken what did not belong to us, or damaged someone else's property out of unkindness or carelessness,
when we have refused out of spite to share or lend to another,
Lord, have mercy,

When we have not kept our word to another, deceived, cheated or been ungenerous in reply,
when we have not listened to what another says, or when we have been preoccupied with our own concerns,
Lord, have mercy.

When we have ignored the needs of others, not appreciated them or helped them to grow, or when we have just disregarded their feelings,
when we have not been gentle or approachable, but harsh, abrasive, cynical,
Lord, have mercy.

When we have not forgiven or been generous to people who upset us;
when we have harboured grudges and resentment, or when we have
    hardened our hearts, made fun of others, or upset their feelings,
Lord, have mercy.

When we have taken people for granted at work or at home,
when we have not given enough time or attention to family, or to others
    who look to us for support,
Lord, have mercy.

When we have been unjust in use of authority, threatened someone or
    bullied them,
when we have used power or position for selfish ends, not as service of
    others,
when we have betrayed the trust others have placed in us,
Lord, have mercy.

For all our failures to love our neighbour as ourselves,
Lord have mercy.

When we have wasted our talents and the time God has given us, in work
    or recreation,
when we have been lazy in work or other commitments,
Lord, have mercy.

When we have been careless in use of material things, or misused them,
when we have been irresponsible stewards of God's gifts and his creation,
Lord, have mercy.

When we have failed to honour our bodies as temples of your Holy Spirit;
when we have used food, drink, drugs or anything else to run away from
    our real selves, other people and from you;
when we have misused our sexuality for selfish purposes and not as a sign
    of our love for another,
Lord, have mercy.

When we have let moodiness, bad temper, impatience, rivalry or ill-will
    prevent us seeing good in others,
when we have taken advantage of another, or used them for our
    own ends,
Lord, have mercy.

When we have let pride, ambition, or social appearances blind us to truth
and justice,
when we have been greedy or impatient to have what we want and failed
in humility to seek what God wants of us,
Lord, have mercy.

For all our failures to live as children of God,
Lord have mercy.

When we have put our self before God, missed Mass or failed to keep
times of prayer through laziness or ill-will,
when we have failed to make sufficient space in our lives to listen to God,
or to seek him in prayer,
Lord, have mercy.

When we have failed to make an effort to deepen our faith by reading,
and thinking,
when we have not tried to live out our faith as an example and sign of
hope to others,
when we have denied God, or through cowardice run away from him,
been deaf to our conscience or not persevered in seeking right rather
than wrong,
Lord, have mercy.

For all our failures to love God with all our heart and soul and strength,
Lord have mercy.

Lord Jesus, you came to call sinners: give us strength to turn away from
temptation and sin.
Lord have mercy.

You heal the wounds of sin and division: heal the weaknesses which lead
us into sin and to lack of friendship with others.
Lord have mercy.

You pray for us with your Father: guide us, help us to repair the damage
our sins have done to others, and renew our lives in your friendship.
Lord have mercy.

Ten Commandments

God said: I am the Lord your God, who brought you out of slavery:

1 You shall have no other gods except me;
2 You shall not speak the name of the Lord to misuse it;
3 Keep the Sabbath holy;
4 Honour your father and mother;
5 You shall not kill;
6 You shall not commit adultery;
7 You shall not steal;
8 You shall not swear falsely against your neighbour;
9 You shall not covet your neighbour's wife;
10 You shall not covet your neighbour's possessions.

Six Chief Commandments of the Church

1 To keep Sundays and Holy Days of Obligation holy by attending Mass and resting from servile works;
2 To keep the days of fasting and abstinence appointed by the Church.
3 To go to Confession at least once a year;
4 To receive Holy Communion at least once a year at Easter or thereabouts.
5 To contribute to the support of our pastors;
6 Not to marry within the proscribed degrees of kindred without dispensation.

Seven Corporal Works of Mercy

1 To feed the hungry;
2 To give drink to the thirsty;
3 To clothe the naked;
4 To shelter the homeless;
5 To visit the sick;
6 To visit those in prison;
7 To bury the dead.

Seven Spiritual Works of Mercy

1 To counsel the doubtful;
2 To instruct the ignorant;
3 To admonish sinners;
4 To comfort the afflicted;
5 To forgive offences;
6 To bear wrongs patiently;
7 To pray for the living and the dead.

Seven Deadly Sins	*Seven Contrary Virtues*
Pride	Humility
Covetousness	Liberality
Lust	Chastity
Anger	Meekness
Gluttony	Temperance
Envy	Brotherly love
Sloth	Diligence

Fruits of the Spirit

You were called to freedom, brothers and sisters; only do not use your freedom as an opportunity for self-indulgence, but through love become servants of one another.

Live by the Spirit and do not gratify the desires of the flesh. For what the flesh desires is opposed to the Spirit, and what the Spirit desires is opposed to the flesh; for these are opposed to prevent you from doing what you want.

Now the works of the flesh are obvious: fornication, impurity, licentiousness, idolatry, sorcery, enmities, strife, jealousy, anger, quarrels, dissensions, factions, envy, drunkenness, carousing and things like these. I am warning you as I warned you before: those who do such things will not inherit the kingdom of God.

By contrast the fruit of the Spirit is love, joy, peace, patience, kindness, generosity, faithfulness, gentleness, and self-control. If we live by the Spirit, let us also be guided by the Spirit.

Galatians 5.13; 16–17; 19–23; 25

The Rite of Confession

Greeting

The priest welcomes you and you both make the Sign of the Cross:

**In the name of the Father, and of the Son,
and of the Holy Spirit.
Amen.**

The priest may give you a blessing in these or similar words:

> May the Lord be in your heart and help you to confess your sins with
> true sorrow.

Confession of sins

Say when you last went to Confession and anything else which may
help the priest understand your situation. Tell him your sins simply
and briefly; you may mention any special difficulties you have living
the Christian life. The priest will try to help you, if necessary, with
questions and advice.

He will then ask you to do something as a sign of sorrow for your
sins or to make good some of the wrong which has been done. He
may ask you to say a prayer or perform some other spiritual work;
he may ask you to do some act of kindness or of self-denial.

Act of contrition

The priest asks you to say a prayer of sorrow. You may use your own words or say one of the following prayers:

O my God, because you are so good
I am very sorry that I have sinned against you,
and by the help of your grace
I will try not to sin again;
through the love of Jesus Christ our Lord.

Lord Jesus, you chose to be called the friend of sinners;
by your saving death and resurrection
free me from my sins.
Let your peace take root in my heart
and bring forth a harvest
of love, holiness and truth.

Lord Jesus, you are the Lamb of God
who takes away the sins of the world;
through the grace of the Holy Spirit
restore me to friendship with your Father,
cleanse me from every stain of sin
in the blood you shed for me,
and raise me to new life
for the glory of your name.

My God, I am sorry for my sins with all my heart:
in choosing to do wrong and in failing to do good,
I have sinned against you whom I should love above all else.
I firmly intend with your help to do penance,
to sin no more and to avoid whatever leads me into sin.
Our Saviour Jesus Christ suffered and died for me:
in his name, my God, have mercy.

Absolution

The priest extends his hand over your head and says:

God, the Father of mercies,
through the death and resurrection of his Son
has reconciled the world to himself
and sent the Holy Spirit among us
for the forgiveness of sins;
through the ministry of the Church,
may God give you pardon and peace.
And I absolve you from your sins
in the name of the Father, and of the Son, and of the Holy Spirit.

You say: **Amen.**

Thanksgiving and dismissal

The priest may invite you to give thanks to God in these or
similar words:

> V. Give thanks to the Lord, for he is good.
> R. For his mercy endures for ever.

He may say the following:

> May the Passion of our Lord Jesus,
> the intercession of the Blessed Virgin Mary and of all the saints,
> whatever good you do and suffering you endure,
> heal your sins,
> help you to grow in holiness,
> and reward you with eternal life.
> Amen.

He then dismisses you with these or similar words:

> The Lord has freed you from your sins.
> Go in peace and pray for me.

V I: Prayers in Sickness and in Death

Prayers for the Sick and Suffering

The world is full of pain; each of us has a share; for some it is a slight burden, for others it is crushing. But every Christian can turn it into a blessing if he seeks Christ's companionship in his sufferings. Then suffering becomes a new point of fellowship with Jesus who himself suffered for us. St Paul teaches that our own suffering lived out with faith and hope in Jesus even plays a part in the world's redemption as we fill up what is left over of the suffering of Christ. Suffering does not, of course, cease to be painful; but it becomes fruitful; and fellowship with Christ on the cross helps us to find new strength, a way by which our hearts are more fully purified from selfishness and able to grow towards perfect love.

adapted from William Temple

It is worth remembering that a sick person may need someone to pray with them, or for them, and someone unconscious can still hear and be aware of those around them. People will often feel frightened by the unknown, and when they may not feel able to pray themselves, they may be more grateful than they can say for the faith of another who can hope in God's love for everyone. God does not want people to suffer, and even when there is no hope of recovery in a medical sense, we still believe God wants them to be saved from the spiritual anguish which confronts someone facing death. As a sign of the Church's hope for the sick and dying, there is the Sacrament of the Sick. Any Catholic has the right to receive the sacraments and a priest should be invited to visit and bring the sacrament to someone who is seriously ill, especially when there is a danger of death. In any case a sick person may wish to receive sacramental absolution in Confession and Holy Communion.

Father, your Son accepted our sufferings to teach us the virtue of patience in human illness. Hear the prayers we offer for our sick brother/sister. May all who suffer pain, illness or disease realize that they have been chosen to be saints and know that they are joined to Christ in his suffering for the salvation of the world.

Pastoral Care of the Sick

Merciful Lord of life and health, look upon our loved one who is sick. Renew his/her strength, and restore him/her to health according to your will. In time of weakness give him/her the renewal of your Spirit and the upholding power of your love; and as all things work together for good to them that love you, so we ask you to pour out your love in his/her heart so that out of this weakness he/she may grow stronger in your grace; through Jesus Christ our Lord.

Prayers for Family Worship

Holy Redeemer, we pray that you will bring to this servant of yours the grace of your Holy Spirit. May it be a healing remedy for all his/her ills; bind up his wounds; forgive his/her sins; rid him/her of all anguish of mind and body. Restore to him/her in your mercy the full health of his/her mind and body, so that he/she will be well again and able to take up his/her work and duties of life again.

Roman rite

For a sick child

God of love, ever caring, ever strong, stand by us in our time of need. Watch over your child _____ who is sick; look after him/her in every danger, and grant him/her your healing and peace. We ask this through Jesus Christ our Lord.

Pastoral Care of the Sick

We ask you not, O Lord, to rid us of pain; but grant in your mercy that our pain may be free from waste, unfettered by rebellion against your will, unsoiled by thought of ourselves, but purified by love and ennobled by devotion to your Kingdom; through the mercies of your only Son, our Lord.

Lord, teach me the art of patience while I am well, and give me the use of it when I am sick. In that day either lighten my burden or strengthen my back. In my health I have so often discovered my weakness, presuming on my own strength: make me to be strong in my sickness when I rely solely on your assistance.

Thomas Fuller

Lord, we pray for all who are weighed down with the mystery of suffering. Reveal yourself to them as the God of love who bears all our sufferings yourself. Grant that we may know that suffering borne in fellowship with you is not a waste or frustration, but can be turned to goodness and blessing, something greater than if we had never suffered, through him who on the cross suffered rejection and hatred, loneliness and despair, agonizing pain and physical death, and rose victorious from the dead, conquering and to conquer, even Jesus Christ our Lord.

George Appleton

Prayers for the Dying and for the Departed

Each of us has over the course of a life to make friends with death; we have to be like St Francis who added the verse to his Canticle of the Sun greeting death as his sister. We meet death in different ways during our lives, almost every day seeing its effects on the television or in newsprint. But its immediate impact, when we meet it in the death of someone close to us, is no less agonizing for all that. It is for all of us the final test of faith and hope, since the only thing that can give us hope is the resurrection of Jesus from the dead. But the love that we can share with a dying person flowing from that faith is a real source of encouragement at a time when they could feel most alone. As is the case in sickness, a dying person may need us to pray the prayers they can no longer say for themselves. Such prayers are best when they are very simple, well-known prayers like the Lord's Prayer or the Rosary.

Heaven is for us all our true home: St Augustine said 'You have made us for yourself and our hearts are restless until they rest in you.'

For the dying

O Lord Jesus Christ, in your last agony you commended your spirit into the hands of your heavenly Father; have mercy upon the sick and dying: may death be to them the gate of everlasting life, and give them the assurance of your abiding presence even in the dark valley; for you are the resurrection and the life.

Sarum Primer

O Living God, in Jesus Christ you were laid in the tomb at the evening hour, and so sanctified the grave to be a bed of hope for your people. Grant us courage and faith to die daily to our sin and pride, that even as this flesh and blood decays, our lives still may grow in you, that at our last day our dying may be done so well that we live in you for ever.

Compline prayer

Grant, Lord, that we may not set our mind on earthly things but love
the things of heaven; and that even now, while we are placed among
things that are passing away, we may cleave to the things that shall abide;
through Jesus Christ our Lord.

Leonine Sacramentary

Give me your grace, good Lord, to make death no stranger to me. Give
me, good Lord, a longing to be with you, not for the avoiding of the
calamities of this wretched world; nor so much for the avoiding of the
pains of purgatory, nor the pains of hell either, nor so much for the
attaining of the joys of heaven (as far as concerns my own comfort),
but for very love of you.

adapted from St Thomas More

O my blessed and glorious creator, you have fed me all my life long, and
redeemed me from all evil; seeing it is your merciful pleasure to take me
out of this frail body, and to wipe away all tears from my eyes, and all
sorrows from my heart, I do with all humility and willingness consent
and submit myself wholly to your sacred will. My most loving redeemer,
into your saving and everlasting arms I commend my spirit; I am ready,
my dear Lord, and earnestly expect and long for your good pleasure.
Come quickly, and receive the soul of your servant who trusts in you.

Henry Vaughan

Bring us, O Lord God, at our last awakening into the house and gate of
heaven, to enter into that gate and dwell in that house, where there shall
be no darkness nor dazzling, but one equal light; no noise nor silence,
but one equal music; no fears nor hopes, but one equal possession; no
ends nor beginnings, but one equal eternity; in the habitations of your
glory and dominion, world without end.

John Donne

O Lord, you have made us very small, and we bring our years to an
end like a tale that is told; help us to remember that beyond our brief
day is the eternity of your love.

Reinhold Niebuhr

O God, early in the morning I cry to you.
Help me to pray and to concentrate my thoughts on you:
I cannot do this alone.
In me there is darkness, but with you there is light;
I am lonely, but you do not leave me.
I am feeble in heart, but with you there is help;
I am restless, but with you there is peace.
In me there is bitterness, but with you there is patience;
I do not understand your ways,
but you know the way wherein I shall walk.
Restore me to liberty, and enable me so to live now
that I may answer before you and before me.
Lord, whatever this day may bring,
your name be praised.

> Dietrich Bonhoeffer,
> *while awaiting execution by the Nazis*

Into your hands, O Lord, I commend my spirit.
Lord Jesus, receive my soul.

Commendation

This form of prayer is said at the time of death or when it seems near.

Go forth upon your journey, Christian soul. Go from this world. Go in
the name of God the Father almighty, who created you; in the name of
Jesus Christ our Lord, who suffered for you; in the name of the Holy
Spirit, who was given to you. Go in the name of Mary, God's holy and
glorious Virgin Mother; in the name of blessed Joseph. Go in the name
of angels and archangels, of thrones and dominations, in the name of
patriarchs and prophets, of the holy apostles and evangelists, of the holy
martyrs, confessors, monks and hermits, of the holy virgins, and of all
the saints of God. May peace be your home this day and paradise your
abode; through Christ our Lord.

Make speed to help him/her saints of God; come forth to meet him/her, angels of the Lord. Receive his/her soul and present him/her before the face of the Most High.

May Christ receive you who has called you, and may angels bear you into the bosom of Abraham.

Eternal rest grant unto him/her, O Lord, and let perpetual light shine upon him/her. May he/she rest in peace.

May the angels lead you into paradise, the martyrs receive you at your coming, and bring you into the holy city, Jerusalem. May choirs of angels sing you welcome; and there, where Lazarus is poor no longer, may you have eternal rest.

For the dead

May the souls of the faithful departed, through the mercy of God, rest in peace.

Receive, Lord, in tranquillity and peace, the souls of your servants who have departed out of this present life to be with you. Give them the life that knows no age, the good things that do not pass away; through Jesus Christ our Lord.

St Ignatius Loyola

Into your hands, O Lord, we commend the spirit of our loved one, now passing from us into your eternal presence. Lord, receive him/her into your holy keeping in the name of the Father and of the Son and of the Holy Spirit.

Queen Elizabeth I

Remember, O Lord, the souls of your servants who have gone before us marked with the sign of faith and who now slumber and sleep in peace. We ask you in your mercy to grant them and all who rest in Christ a place of refreshment, light and peace; through Jesus Christ our Lord.

from the Roman Canon

Lord God, the glory of all the faithful and life of the just, by the death of whose Son we are redeemed, hear our prayers on behalf of your servant _____ who shared our faith in the mystery of our resurrection in Christ, and grant him/her to receive the eternal reward of heavenly joy; through the same Jesus Christ our Lord.

Hear us, O Lord, as we pray for _____. In your love you gave him/her life, and you have called him/her from this life to be with you. Give him/her the fulfilment of all his/her hopes, the forgiveness of his/her sins, the healing of all the wounds of his/her life, the strengthening of all his/her weakness. May he/she rejoice in the vision of your glory, and in the sure knowledge that now he/she can never be separated from your love. For us who mourn, we ask that you will confirm our faith that, in Christ, we are not separated from those who die in faith, but are still with them a part of your own body which died and rose again. And at the time of our departing, may we be reunited with him/her in the peace and joy of your kingdom.

For those who mourn

O Lord, our God, from whom neither life nor death can separate those who trust in your love, and whose love holds in its embrace your children in this world and the next; so unite us to yourself that in fellowship with you we may always be united to our loved ones whether here or there; give us courage, constancy and hope; through him who died and was buried and rose again for us, Jesus Christ our Lord.

William Temple

We seem to give them back to you, O God, who gave them to us. Yet as you did not lose them in giving, so do we not lose them by their return. Not as the world gives, do you give, O lover of souls. What you give you do not take away, for what is yours is ours also if we are yours. And life is eternal and love immortal, and death is only an horizon, and an horizon is nothing save the limit of our sight. Lift us up, strong Son of God, that we may see further; cleanse our eyes that we may see more clearly;

draw us closer to yourself that we may know ourselves to be nearer to our loved ones who are with you. And while you prepare a place for us, prepare us also for that happy place, that where you are we may be also for evermore.

Bede Jarrett OP

O God, our Father, we know that you are afflicted in all our afflictions; and in our sorrow we come to you now that you may give us the comfort which you alone can give.

Make us to be sure that in perfect wisdom, perfect love, and perfect power you are working ever for the best.

Make us sure that a Father's hand will never cause his child a needless tear.

Make us sure of your love, so that we will be able to accept even that which we cannot understand. Help us today to be thinking not of the darkness of death but of the splendour of life everlasting, for ever in your presence and for ever with you.

Help us still to face life with grace and gallantry; and help us to find courage to go on in the memory that the best tribute we can pay to our loved one is not the tribute of tears, but the constant memory that another has been added to the unseen cloud of witnesses who compass about us.

Comfort and uphold us, strengthen and support us, until we also come to the green pastures which are beside the still waters, and until we meet again those whom we have loved and lost awhile; through Jesus Christ our Lord.

William Barclay

De Profundis

The title is taken from the first two words of the Latin version of Psalm 129(130). It is often used as a devotion for the dead since it is a psalm of repentance, acknowledging the way sin and death go closely together. For that reason it is also a psalm of hope: the God who forgives sin is also a God whose power to save is not hampered by death. We look forward in hope to God like someone waiting for the dawn of a new day.

Out of the depths I cry to you, O Lord.
Lord, hear my voice.
Let your ears be attentive
to the voice of my supplications.

If you, O Lord, should mark iniquities,
Lord, who could stand?
But there is forgiveness with you
so that you may be revered.

I wait for the Lord, my soul waits,
and in his word I hope;
My soul waits for the Lord
more than those who watch for the morning.

O Israel, hope in the Lord!
For with the Lord there is steadfast love,
and with him is great power to redeem.
It is he who will redeem Israel

from all its iniquities.
Eternal rest grant unto them O Lord;
And let perpetual light shine upon them.
May they rest in peace. Amen.

O God, the creator and redeemer of all the faithful, grant to the souls of your faithful departed the remission of all their sins, that through our supplications they may obtain that pardon which they have always desired; through Jesus Christ our Lord, who lives and reigns with you in the unity of the Holy Spirit, one God, world without end.

VII: Prayers for the Christian Year

Advent

The Church's year begins with Advent. God comes to us; he does not
wait for us to reach him. We remember the steps he took to prepare
for the birth of Christ, and think especially of Mary and John the
Baptist. Christ lives in our hearts, and we use Advent as a time to prepare
ourselves for the renewal of his birth in our lives at Christmas. We also
look ahead to when he will come again according to his promise,
the time when all history will be finished and God will establish his
kingdom for ever.

Almighty God, give us grace that we may cast away the works of darkness
and put upon us the armour of light during the time of this mortal life; so
that on the last day, when your Son Jesus Christ will come again in majesty
to judge the living and the dead, we may rise to life everlasting; through
his name.

adapted from The Book of Common Prayer

Stir up our hearts, we beseech you, O Lord, that we may prepare the way for
your only begotten Son; so that by his advent we may be enabled to serve
you with pure hearts and minds; through the same Jesus Christ our Lord.
Gelasian Sacramentary

Almighty God, in the wisdom of your providence you have made all ages
serve as a preparation for the kingdom of your Son. Make our hearts ready
to behold the brightness of your glory. Wake us from our sleep, renew your
life within us, deepen our faith in spiritual realities, stir up our love for
them and restore our hope. Open our eyes as we wait for the dawn of your
heavenly kingdom that we may live in peace with one another; through our
Saviour and Lord, Jesus Christ.

Collection of Prayers by John Hunter

O Antiphons for the last days of Advent

These antiphons, said with the Magnificat at Evening Prayer, are a way of giving a biblical shape to our Christmas preparations.

17 December

O Wisdom, proceeding from the mouth of the Most High God and reaching to the ends of creation, mightily and sweetly disposing all things: come and teach us the way of prudence.

18 December

O Adonai, Leader of the House of Israel, who appeared to Moses in the fire of the burning bush and gave him the Law on Mount Sinai: come and redeem us by your outstretched arm.

19 December

O Root of Jesse, standing as an ensign to the nations of the earth, before whom rulers will stand dumb, to whom all peoples will pray: come and deliver us; do not delay.

20 December

O Key of David and Sceptre of the House of Israel, where you open no one will close, and where you close no one will open: come and lead your people from captivity where they sit in darkness and in the shadow of death.

21 December

O Dawn in the East, splendour of eternal light and Sun of Justice: come and give light to those who sit in darkness and in the shadow of death.

22 December

O King of the nations, desire of human hearts, the cornerstone bringing all together into one: come and save us whom you have fashioned out of clay.

23 December

O Emmanuel, our King and Lawgiver, hope of the earth and Saviour of mankind: come and save us, O Lord our God.

Christmas

At Christmas we marvel that the maker of all things and source of all life himself lived a human life like ours in everything except sin. The human birth of God is the foundation of our salvation from sin and death; it is also the start of a new way of living by means of which we are raised up to share the fullness of life in Christ. We become by grace what Jesus is by nature, 'participants of the divine nature' as the Second Letter of Peter puts it (2 Peter 1.4). It is a time to be thankful for the gift and mystery of life, and to remember that all human life is sacred, a gift to us to be shared with others as God shared his life with us. New Year's Day is also the Feast of Mary the Mother of God; it is a day to celebrate the part Mary played in the life of Christ, not just in giving birth to Jesus, but also in bringing him up and teaching him the first lessons of life. On the Sunday after Christmas we remember the Holy Family and the precious part a family plays in human life. It gives us our first experience of human life, of trust, love and joy. It provides the ground on which all our personal relationships will be built. Epiphany is celebrated on 6 January, the Twelfth Day of Christmas. It commemorates the first events which revealed the divine power of Jesus. In the first place it recalls the journey of the wise men from the East; but in ancient times it also celebrated the Baptism of Christ and the Marriage at Cana. The Sunday after Epiphany is now the Feast of the Baptism of the Lord with which the Christmas season ends.

The king of peace is glorified, the sight of whose face is the desire of the whole earth.

Vespers antiphon

Lord Jesus, born at this time,
a little child for love of us;
be born in me that I may be a little child in love of you;
and hang on your love trustfully, lovingly, peacefully,
hushing all my cares in love of you.

Lord Jesus, sweeten every thought of mine with the sweetness of your love. Give me a deep love of you that nothing may be too hard for me to bear for love of you.

E. B. Pusey

Most merciful and loving God, through your will Jesus Christ our Lord humbled himself that he might exalt creation; he became flesh that he might restore your image in us and was born of the Virgin that he might uphold the lowly. Grant unto us the inheritance of the meek, perfect in us your likeness and bring us at last to your beauty, that we may glorify your grace; through Jesus Christ our Lord.

Gelasian Sacramentary

Grant us, O heavenly Father, such love and wonder at your Son's birth that we may come with shepherds, wise men and pilgrims to adore him, the King of Heaven. May we offer him the gift of a pure heart, and the poverty of our spirit to be enriched by his mercy and love. As we see God living our human life, so may we rejoice in the full vision of his glory in heaven.

adapted from James Ferguson

Almighty and everlasting Lord, you made known the incarnation of your Son by the shining of a star, which led the wise men to behold and adore your majesty. Grant that the star of your righteousness may always shine in our hearts, and that, as our treasure, we may give ourselves and all we possess to your service; through Christ our Lord.

Gelasian Sacramentary

New Year

An old custom used to be to give thanks for the old year and pray for blessing on the new. At an early date, the Roman Church kept the day as a feast of Mary and dedicated the new year to the intercession of the Mother of God. It is also observed now as the World Day of Prayer for Peace.

O God of infinite mercy and generosity, we give you thanks for all the good things you have given us over the past year, and ask you in your kindness that, as you have answered the prayers of those who turn to you in faith, so you will never leave us but prepare us for the rewards of eternal life; through Jesus Christ our Lord.

Lord of creation, in whose power are all times and seasons, bless this year and crown it with your goodness. Keep your Church in peace, grant us every blessing and lead us to our eternal home, where you reign for ever and ever.

Almighty God, in whose hands lies the destiny of mankind and of the world, let not our hopes perish, nor our sacrifices be in vain.
Holy Spirit and giver of life, give us grace to root out from our life the bitterness of ancient wrongs and the desire to be avenged for the betrayals of long ago. Save us from the tyranny of history and set us free to serve each other attentively and live the present as a gift of new life. In the power of our redemption by you we believe that all our sins of yesterday are forgiven by your love; grant us the grace and courage now to give and receive the forgiveness which alone can heal the wounds which remain. Draw us towards your loving kindness and guide us in the way of peace.

Anonymous

Lent

Lent is the traditional time of fasting for Christians. For Christians it is a way of preparing to celebrate the Lord's Passion and death, so that by coming to grips with the sin in our lives which killed Jesus we may share more fully in the new life he won for us by conquering death. We can observe Lent by fasting, prayer and almsgiving or works of charity. Grand gestures are not called for: only the desire to do something to make more room for God and for other people in our lives; in short, to try to be less selfish. Lent is a season of repentance, of returning to God. It is a good idea to make your Confession at this time, which Catholics are encouraged to do at least once every year. It is also a season of renewal, of opening ourselves up to God's grace and seeking more generously to do his will.

Lent starts on Ash Wednesday, when ashes are blessed and put on people's heads at Mass. Dust and ashes are a traditional sign of mourning and repentance, since they remind us of the dust from which we were made and to which we return at death. We remember our mortality and weakness so that we may receive God's grace which gives life to our mortal bodies. Lent is kept for forty days and nights, imitating our Lord's fasting in the desert after his Baptism. Sundays and feasts are exempted from the fast, which thus lasts for five weeks of Lent and Holy Week until Holy Thursday. Good Friday, like Ash Wednesday, is a day of fasting and abstinence, when adult Catholics not only eat less but also abstain from meat.

Almighty God, through whose Word you work out the reconciliation of mankind, grant that by this holy fast of Lent, in prayer and good works, we may listen more attentively to your Word in our hearts, and grow in obedience to you and in friendship with our neighbour; through Jesus Christ our Lord.

Gelasian Sacramentary

Direct our hearts to you, Lord, so that we may follow you more closely this Lent and all the days of our life; in all our needs we turn to you for the help of your grace, and ask you to give us strength to work for the things we ask for in faith, through Jesus Christ our Lord.

Protect us, Lord, from becoming entangled in the cares of this life, or absorbed by too much pleasure in it. Give us strength to resist all that distracts us from living daily towards you, patience to endure all the challenges on our path, and constancy to persevere to the end; through Jesus Christ our Lord.

adapted from Thomas à Kempis

Christ suffered for us,
leaving us an example that we should follow his steps.
He committed no sin,
and no deceit was found in his mouth.
When he was abused, he did not return abuse;
when he suffered, he did no threaten;
but he entrusted himself to the one who judges justly.
He himself bore our sins in his body on the Cross,
so that, free from sins, we might live for righteousness;
by his wounds we have been healed.
For we were going astray like sheep,
but now we have returned to the shepherd and guardian of our souls.

adapted from 1 Peter 2.21–25

Holy Week

The last week before Easter follows the path of our Lord's Passion
from his triumphant entry into Jerusalem as the Messiah on Palm
Sunday to his rejection, crucifixion and burial on Good Friday.
Palm Sunday is also called Passion Sunday because in place of the
Gospel one of the Passions of the Lord is read. On Thursday Mass is
celebrated in the evening to commemorate the Last Supper. It is not
said again until the Easter Sunday, but there are special services to
mark the three days known as the Triduum of the Lord's Passion and
Resurrection. After the Mass of the Lord's Supper there is a time of
solemn adoration of the Blessed Sacrament until midnight, when
Friday is given over to the memory of Christ's betrayal, suffering
and death. On the Friday afternoon, after the time of his death on
the cross, the Church gathers to listen to the Passion story again,
traditionally from St John's Gospel, which presents the Cross as a sign
of Christ's glory as the true king of the world, and we join the Lord
in intercession for the whole world. The cross is then lifted up for
veneration and the figure of the suffering Christ adored. The Triduum
culminates on the Saturday night with the Easter Vigil recalling the
long history of salvation leading from creation to the resurrection
of the Lord.

Saviour of the world, who by your Cross and precious death have
redeemed us, have mercy on us, we humbly beseech you, O Lord.

Lord Jesus, you gave yourself for me. Give me the fullness of your love,
that for all your love, with your love, I may love you.

Jesus Christ, give us patience and faith and hope as we kneel at the foot of your Cross, and hold fast to it. Teach us by your Cross that, however ill the world may go, the Father so loved us that he did not spare you, but received the offering of your life so that we might live through you and in you and for you, who are the resurrection and the life.

Charles Kingsley

Make me cheerful under every cross, for love of your Cross. Take from me all that displeases you or hinders your love in me, that I may deeply love you. Melt me with your love, that I may be all love, and with my whole being love you.

E. B. Pusey

Let this mind be in you which was also in Christ Jesus,
who, though he was in the form of God,
did not count equality with God something to be exploited,
but emptied himself, taking the form of a servant,
being born in human likeness.
And being found in human form, he humbled himself
and became obedient unto death, even death on a cross.
Therefore God also highly exalted him
and gave him the name that is above every name,
so that at the name of Jesus every knee should bend,
in heaven and on earth and under the earth,
and every tongue confess that Jesus Christ is Lord,
to the glory of God the Father

Philippians 2.5–11

Easter

Easter, the celebration of the resurrection of Christ and of our new life in him, lasts for fifty days. As a way of showing that time has begun again and creation made new, it lasts seven times seven days, a whole week of weeks, and culminates in the descent of the Holy Spirit on the disciples at Pentecost. It includes the Ascension of the Lord to heaven on the fortieth day, the Thursday in the sixth week of Easter. In the first eight days, until the second Sunday of Easter, we recall the appearances of our Lord to the disciples after his resurrection.

Meditation on the Easter appearances of Jesus
We adore you, Christ, Son of the living God.
In triumph you rose from the grave and bore in your hands the keys of
    death and hell; we rejoice in your almighty power and glory. Raise us
    up with you above all earthly desires, inspire us with thoughts of joy,
    hope and love.
Enter within our hearts and say 'Peace be to you.'
Give us grace to see you with the eyes of our understanding so that we
    may know you walking by our side on our earthly pilgrimage. Come
    to us and dwell within us; stay with us and make yourself known to us
    in the scriptures and in the breaking of bread.
Teach us, as we sail our boat through the darkness of this life, to see you
    standing on the everlasting shore of peace and let us come to you
    across the waters. Give us grace to rise with you and leave all for sake
    of you that we may be made like you and that we may follow you
    wherever you go.

adapted from a Treasury of Devotion

Eternal God of peace and consolation, who brought again from the dead our Lord Jesus Christ, the great shepherd of the sheep, through the blood of the everlasting covenant, make us fruitful in all good works to do your will and work in us what is acceptable in your sight. Sanctify us wholly and keep our spirit, soul and body faultless for the coming of your Son, our Lord Jesus Christ. You are faithful and have promised, and your promise you will surely bring to pass. Yours be all praise and honour and glory.

based on Hebrews 13.20

Ascension

When Jesus ascended to heaven, according to the Gospel account, he returned to his Father to sit at his right hand in glory until the end of time. But he also promised not to leave us like orphans. He remains with us, more closely now because he is not just physically present in the world any longer: no space or time separates us from him. He is the Lord of all creation, and guides everything to fulfilment in the Kingdom of God.

Jesus also told the disciples to wait and pray for the Holy Spirit. In the days between Ascension and Pentecost, then, we too pray especially for the power of God's Spirit to fill our hearts and minds so that we can do his will and carry on the work of the Gospel. The hymns of the Holy Spirit could be said as part of this preparation (see pages 177–179).

O King of glory, Lord of hosts, who rose today in triumph above the heavens: do not leave us orphans, but send us your Holy Spirit, the Spirit of Truth, promised us by the Father. Alleluia.

St Bede

Grant, almighty God, that we who believe that your only begotten Son, our Redeemer, ascended this day into heaven may also have our hearts fixed on heavenly things; through the same Lord, Jesus Christ.
O Lord Jesus Christ, who after your resurrection from the dead gloriously ascended into heaven: grant us the help of your loving kindness, that according to your promise you may ever dwell with us on earth, and we with you in heaven, where with the Father and the Holy Spirit you live and reign one God, for ever and ever.

Gelasian Sacramentary

Lord Jesus Christ, who in leaving us promised that you would come again and take us to be with you for ever: grant that in our communion with you now our souls may ever thirst for that time when we shall behold you in your glory; who live and reign with the Father and the Holy Spirit world without end.

Liturgy of the Catholic Apostolic Church

Pentecost

The fiftieth day of Easter is the day when the Holy Spirit came in power on the disciples and changed weak and timid men and women into people who would carry the Gospel to the ends of the earth. It is the birthday of the Church, the Body of Christ, which still lives his divine life in the world. By Baptism we are, as it were, limbs of a single body living a single life, the life of the Spirit, just as Jesus himself lived it during his life on earth. The Holy Spirit that had overshadowed Mary and enabled her to be the Mother of God enables us to be bearers of Christ, whatever we do in his name.

Lord Jesus, all power is given you in heaven and on earth. Transform our understanding and our will by the gift of your Holy Spirit; may our minds and bodies be subject to your Spirit and all our affections and desires be directed towards your pure and holy will, to the praise and glory of your sovereign grace.

Ludoricus Vives

See also the hymns, prayers and litany of the Holy Spirit (pages 177–179 and pages 188–190).

After Pentecost

Pentecost is followed by three solemnities, the Holy Trinity, Corpus Christi, and the Sacred Heart. The feast of the Holy Trinity invites us to stand back from the series of feasts which mark out the main part of the Christian Year; in it we worship the mystery of the one God who works through the life of Christ and the saints as Father, Son and Holy Spirit. We worship the Father and Spirit whom we come to know through Jesus Christ. The basic shape of our faith in the Trinity is spelled out in the creeds of the Church.

Corpus Christi is a celebration of the mystery of the Eucharist we celebrate at Mass, the sacrament in which Jesus remains with us to feed us and lead us on our journey to heaven. On Holy Thursday we celebrate the Lord's Supper in the shadow of the Cross and Passion. At Corpus Christi we do so rejoicing in the full glory of the resurrection, looking forward to its fulfilment in the feast of heavenly life.

The feast of the Sacred Heart of Jesus is a beautiful feast celebrating the everlasting mercy of God. Jesus turns no one away; no sin is beyond redemption for those who truly repent. We do not have to earn God's love, only open our hands and our hearts to receive it in full measure.

At the end of the Church's Year, on 1 November, comes the feast of All Saints where we celebrate our communion with all those who have been made perfect and already share the joy of heaven. They are too many to be named; their lives may have gone unnoticed to all except their creator. They may have sinned greatly, but their sins have been wiped away. They pray for us as we follow them and look forward to rejoicing with them in heaven.

The following day, 2 November, the Church sets a special day of prayer aside for the souls of the departed. While the saints pray for us, we should pray for the dead, that their sins be forgiven, their spiritual wounds healed, and all their weaknesses made strong so that they may be made ready by God's grace for the joy of heaven.

The last Sunday before Advent is the Feast of Christ, the King of all creation. Here we celebrate the one who will come again at the end of all things to establish the eternal Kingdom of God in which all things will be subject to the authority of Christ and God will be all in all.

VIII: Prayers to Our Lady

When we pray to Mary, we pray to her as the mother of our Lord Jesus Christ. We pray to her as we would ask any other Christian to pray for us: Mary is herself one of the faithful redeemed by Jesus Christ. But, as the mother of Christ, we believe she is also the mother of the Church, which is the Body of Christ. This gives her a special place in the life of the Church, a special place in its prayer and devotion. For just as she was the mother of our Saviour, so we pray that she will help and support our own life of faith with a mother's love.

All the prayers in this section make a link between Mary and the mystery of the birth of Jesus and of our redemption by him.

The Angelus

This devotion was traditionally said at the beginning and end of
the working day and at its middle. It was a simple way for ordinary
Christians to make the day holy and to imitate the regular daily prayer
of the Liturgy of the Hours celebrated by monks and priests. To help
people observe the devotion in common, wherever they were at
work, the bells of the church would be rung.

As a form of prayer it simply recalls the incarnation of Jesus
and the part Mary played in accepting the invitation of the angel.
Each verse and response is followed by a *Hail Mary*, and the whole
devotion is completed with a prayer in which we see our own lives
mirrored in hers: through the Gospel we too have received the
promise of salvation by Jesus; we are saved by sharing in the mystery
of his birth, death and resurrection. It is a reminder that each of us
is invited to bring Christ into the world through our own lives.
During Eastertide the *Regina Caeli* is said instead.

The angel of the Lord declared unto Mary;
And she conceived by the Holy Spirit. Hail Mary . . .

Behold the handmaid of the Lord;
Be it done unto me according to your word. Hail Mary . . .

The Word was made flesh;
And dwelt among us. Hail Mary . . .

> V. Pray for us, O holy Mother of God:
> R. That we may be made worthy of the promises of Christ.

Pour forth, we beseech you, O Lord, your grace into our hearts,
so that we, to whom the incarnation of Christ your Son, was made
known by the message of an angel, may, by his Passion and Cross,
be brought to the glory of his resurrection; through the same
Christ our Lord.

Antiphons to Our Lady

These antiphons are part of a traditional devotion to Mary used in the Prayer of the Church after Compline. They reflect the scriptural imagery which has inspired generations of Christians in their contemplation of the Mother of God. The antiphons are followed by their traditional verses and prayers, which reflect the different moods of the Christian Year.

Alma Redemptoris Mater
from Advent Sunday to the Feast of the Presentation (February 2nd)

Alma redemptoris mater,
Quae pervia caeli porta manes, et stella maris,
Succurre cadenti, surgere qui curat, populo;
Tu quae genuisti, natura mirante,
Tuum sanctum genitorem,
Virgo prius ac posterius,
Gabrielis ab ore sumens illud Ave,
Peccatorum miserere.

Mother of Christ, hear thou thy people's cry.
Star of the sea and portal of the sky.
Sinking we strive and call to thee for aid.
Mother of him who thee from nothing made,
O by that joy which Gabriel brought to thee,
Thou, Virgin first and last, let us thy mercy see.

> *During Advent*
> V. The angel of the Lord declared unto Mary.
> R. And she conceived by the Holy Spirit.

Pour forth, we beseech you, O Lord, your grace into our hearts, so that we, to whom the incarnation of Christ, your Son, was made known by the message of an angel, may, by his Passion and Cross, be brought to the glory of his resurrection; through Christ our Lord.

V. After childbirth, you remained a virgin.
R. Pray for us, O Mother of God.

O God, through the fruitfulness of the Virgin Mary you have given us the reward of eternal salvation; grant that we may always know the power of her intercession through whom we have been counted worthy to receive the author of all life, the same Jesus Christ our Lord.

Ave Regina Caelorum
from the Presentation to Easter

Ave regina caelorum,
Ave domina angelorum;
Salve radix, salve porta,
Ex qua mundo lux est orta;
Gaude, Virgo gloriosa,
Super omnes speciosa;
Vale, O valde decora,
Et pro nobis Christum exora.
Hail, O queen of heaven enthroned,
Hail, as queen of angels owned.
Root of Jesse, gate of morn,
whence the world's true light was born.
Glorious Virgin, joy to thee,
the loveliest in heaven to see.
Fairest thou, where all are fair,
plead with Christ our sins to spare.

V. Grant that I may give you worthy praise, O holy Virgin.
R. Give me strength against all your enemies.

Give us help in our weakness, O merciful God, so that as we keep holy the memory of the Mother of God, by the help of her intercession we may be saved from our sins; through Jesus Christ our Lord.

Regina Caeli
from Easter to Pentecost

Regina caeli, laetare, Alleluia,
Quia quem meruisti portare, Alleluia,
Resurrexit, sicut dixit, Alleluia,
Ora pro nobis Deum, Alleluia.

Queen of heaven, rejoice, Alleluia.
For he whom thou didst merit to bear, Alleluia.
Has risen as he said, Alleluia.
Pray for us to God, Alleluia.

> V. Rejoice and be glad O Virgin Mary. Alleluia.
> R. For the Lord has risen indeed. Alleluia.

O God, who by the resurrection of your Son our Lord Jesus Christ
has given joy to the whole world: grant that through the help of his
mother we may obtain the joys of everlasting life; through the same
Jesus Christ our Lord.

The Regina Caeli is said instead of the Angelus during Eastertide.

Salve Regina
from Pentecost to Advent

Salve regina, mater misericordiae;
Vita, dulcedo et spes nostra, salve.
Ad te clamamus, exsules filii Hevae.
Ad te suspiramus gementes et flentes
In hac lacrimarum valle.
Eia ergo, advocata nostra,
Illos tuos misericordes oculos ad nos converte.
Et Jesum, benedictum fructum ventris tui,
Nobis post hoc exsilium ostende.
O clemens, o pia, o dulcis Virgo Maria.

Hail, holy queen, mother of mercy,
Hail our life, our sweetness and our hope;
To thee do we cry, poor banished children of Eve;
To thee do we send up our sighs,
Mourning and weeping in this vale of tears.
Turn then, most gracious advocate,
Thine eyes of mercy towards us;
And after this our exile show unto us
The blessed fruit of thy womb, Jesus.
O clement, O loving, O sweet Virgin Mary.

> V. Pray for us, holy Mother of God:
> R. That we may be made worthy of the promises of Christ.

Almighty and everlasting God, who by the co-operation of the Holy Spirit prepared the body and soul of Mary, the glorious Virgin Mother of God to be a fitting dwelling place of your Son, our Lord Jesus Christ; grant that as we rejoice to keep her memory alive in our hearts, so by her devout prayers we may be delivered from the evils that beset us now and from eternal death; through the same Jesus Christ our Lord.

Sub Tuum Praesidium

The following antiphon is the oldest prayer to the Virgin known
in Latin; it was written shortly after the council of Ephesus in 431,
which affirmed the human birth of the Son of God, and the truth
of the title of Mary as the *Theotokos* or Mother of God.

Sub tuum praesidium confugimus, sancta Dei Genitrix;
Nostras deprecationes ne despicias in necessitatibus,
Sed a periculis cunctis libera nos semper,
Virgo gloriosa et benedicta.

In your loving care we take refuge, O holy Mother of God.
Do not disregard our prayers in the time of our need;
But in every danger set us free,
O glorious and blessed Virgin.

The Memorare

This antiphon was composed by St Bernard and resembles the
antiphons in honour of Mary which have become an established part
of the Church's liturgical prayer. This prayer sounds a more popular
note in that it expresses a direct appeal to Mary's prayer on our behalf.
The combination of contrition and tenderness towards Mary is
characteristic of the twelfth century, the time of its composition.

Remember, O most loving Virgin Mary, that it is a thing unheard of, that
anyone ever had recourse to your protection, implored your help, or
sought your intercession, and was left forsaken. Filled therefore with
confidence in your goodness I fly to you, O Mother, Virgin of virgins.
To you I come, before you I stand, a sorrowful sinner. Despise not my
poor words, O Mother of the Word of God, but graciously hear and
grant my prayer.

> V. Pray for us, Holy Mother of God:
> R. That we may be made worthy of the promises of Christ.

Have mercy on the failings of your faithful people, O Lord, so that we,
who without the help of your grace cannot please you, may be saved
through the intercession of the Mother of our Lord, your Son Jesus Christ.

In the Middle Ages, Mary came to be seen increasingly as someone to whom Christians could turn on their behalf to intercede for them. The prayer of St Francis also reflects mediaeval courtly etiquette in its approach to the Queen of Heaven.

Most glorious, ever virgin, blessed Mother of God, present our prayer to your Son and our God, and plead with him, that through you we may gain salvation.

Hail, holy lady, most holy queen,
ever-virgin Mary, Mother of God,
chosen by the most holy Father in heaven,
and consecrated by him,
with his most holy beloved Son,
and the Holy Spirit the Comforter.
On you descended and in you still remains
all the fullness of grace and every good.
Hail, his palace, his tabernacle, his robe.
Hail, his handmaid and mother.
Hail, all holy virtues,
which, by the grace and inspiration of the Holy Spirit,
are poured into the hearts of the faithful,
so that, faithless no longer,
they may be made faithful servants of God through you.
                                                    St Francis of Assisi

The Magnificat or Song of Mary

This song is taken from the Gospel of Luke, where it is part of the story of Mary's visit to Elizabeth, her reply to the greeting by Elizabeth which we use in the Hail Mary. It draws on several themes of Jewish prayer which we find in the Old Testament. It is used every day at Vespers in the evening prayer of the Church.

My soul magnifies the Lord,

and my spirit rejoices in God my Saviour,

for he has looked with favour on the lowliness of his servant.

Surely, from now on all generations will call me blessed;

for the Mighty One has done great things for me,

and holy is his name.

His mercy is for those who fear him

from generation to generation.

He has shown strength with his arm;

he has scattered the proud in the thoughts of their hearts.

He has brought down the powerful from their thrones,

and lifted up the lowly;

he has filled the hungry with good things,

and sent the rich away empty.

He has helped his servant Israel,

in remembrance of his mercy,

according to the promise he made to our ancestors,

to Abraham and his descendants forever.

Magnificat anima mea Dominum;

Et exultavit spiritus meus in Deo salutari meo.

Quia respexit humilitatem ancillae suae;

ecce enim ex hoc beatam me dicent omnes generationes.

Quia fecit mihi magna, qui potens est;

et sanctum nomen eius.

Et misericordia eius a progenie in progenies

timentibus eum.

Fecit potentiam in bracchio suo;

dispersit superbos mente cordis sui.

Deposuit potentes de sede, et exaltavit humiles.

Esurientes implevit bonis;

et divites dimisit inanes.

Suscepit Israel puerum suum,

recordatus misericordiae suae.

Sicut locutus est ad patres nostros,

Abraham et semini eius in saecula.

Prayers for the Solemnities of Mary

The Solemnity of Mary the Mother of God 1 January

Almighty God, you loved the world so much that you gave your only Son to take our human nature on him and to be born of the Virgin Mary; grant that as we are reborn in him so we may always be supported by the love and prayers of his mother and every day grow in the grace of the Holy Spirit until we are brought to sing your praises with her in heaven; through Jesus Christ our Lord.

The Assumption of the Blessed Virgin Mary 15 August

Almighty and eternal God, you raised the body and soul of the Immaculate Virgin Mary, the Mother of your Son, into the glory of heaven. Grant us the grace to keep our hearts and minds on the things of heaven, that we may one day share with her in glory; through Christ our Lord, who lives and reigns with you in the unity of the Holy Spirit, one God, for ever and ever.

The Immaculate Conception of the Blessed Virgin Mary 8 December

Almighty God, by the Immaculate Conception of the Blessed Virgin Mary you prepared a worthy dwelling place for your Son. As you preserved her from all sin, by her intercession may we be brought to the vision of your beauty and live with you forever; through Christ our Lord.

The Rosary

The Rosary is a simple way of meditating on the life, death and resurrection of Jesus. In saying the Rosary we follow Jesus' life, as it were, in the company of his mother Mary, beginning from her call by God to play her part in the story of our salvation, to the fulfilment of her life in the glory of heaven which we hope to share with her.

The origins of the rosary are ancient; the early monks used to 'count' prayers using a knotted band. Among Catholics, the Rosary we know today developed out of this kind of repetitive prayer as a devotion to Mary. The pattern of prayer copied the Office said by clergy and monks with its 150 psalms. Thus fifteen 'Mysteries' of the Rosary came to be said, each consisting of ten Hail Marys beginning with a Lord's Prayer and ending, like the psalms, with a Glory Be.

Each sequence of ten Hail Marys is known as a 'decade' and a rosary usually consists of five groups of ten beads to count the Hail Marys, separated by a larger bead to mark the Lord's Prayer and Glory Be. In addition there is usually a cross attached to the circle of beads, with a further three small and two large beads. These can be used as a preparation, saying the Creed as well as the prayers used to meditate on one of the Mysteries.

Rosary beads can be simply held in one hand and passed through the fingers one by one, saying the Hail Mary on each of the small beads, with an Our Father to start the series. After a group of ten small beads there is a gap before a large bead; this is a reminder to say the Glory Be. The large bead marks the start of a new decade, with the Lord's Prayer said before the Hail Marys. The process can be repeated until the whole sequence of beads has passed through the fingers. Feeling the beads is often enough to help one return to the work of prayer.

Traditionally the Mysteries of the Rosary have been grouped into three sets of five as listed below, but other events in the life of Jesus and Mary have also been used and the Rosary can easily be adapted to suit personal needs. In the same way anyone is free to say as many or as few prayers with the beads as they feel is right. The rosary can also be used simply for supporting the meditative repetition of the Hail

Mary, or some other prayer, without thinking about anything in particular. It may well be that the prayers can get in the way of the praying, and then it is best to let the touch of the fingers on the beads keep our attention on the mystery, while our mind and heart open out of their own accord to God in quiet.

For like any method of prayer it is there to help, not to enslave. Otherwise even the Rosary will become just a meaningless repetition.

The joyful mysteries

1. The Annunciation

In the sixth month the angel Gabriel was sent by God to a town in Galilee called Nazareth, to a virgin betrothed to a man named Joseph, of the House of David; and the virgin's name was Mary. He went in and said to her, 'Rejoice, so highly favoured! The Lord is with you.' She was deeply disturbed by these words and asked herself what this greeting could mean, but the angel said to her, 'Mary, do not be afraid; you have won God's favour. Listen! You are to conceive and bear a son, and you must name him Jesus. He will be great and will be called Son of the Most High. The Lord God will give him the throne of his ancestor David; he will rule over the House of Jacob for ever and his reign will have no end.' Mary said to the angel, 'But how can this come about, since I am a virgin?' 'The Holy Spirit will come upon you,' the angel answered, 'and the power of the Most High will cover you with its shadow. And so the child will be holy and will be called Son of God. Know this too: your kinswoman Elizabeth has, in her old age, herself conceived a son, and she whom people called barren is now in her sixth month, for nothing is impossible to God.' 'I am the handmaid of the Lord,' said Mary, 'Let what you have said be done to me.' And the angel left her.

Luke 1.26–38

2. The Visitation

Mary set out at that time and went as quickly as she could into the hill country to a town in Judah. She went into Zechariah's house and greeted Elizabeth. Now as soon as Elizabeth heard Mary's greeting, the child leapt in her womb and Elizabeth was filled with the Holy Spirit. She gave a loud cry and said, 'Of all women you are the most blessed, and blessed is the fruit of your womb. Why should I be honoured with a visit from the mother of my Lord? For the moment your greeting reached my ears, the child in my womb leapt for joy. Yes, blessed is she who believed that the promise made to her by the Lord would be fulfilled.'

Luke 1.39–45

3. The birth of our Lord Jesus Christ at Bethlehem

Now at this time Caesar Augustus issued a decree that a census should be made of the whole inhabited world. This census – the first – took place while Quirinius was governor of Syria, and every one went to his own town to be registered. So Joseph set out from the town of Nazareth in Galilee for Judaea, to the town of David called Bethlehem, since he was of David's house and line, in order to be registered together with Mary, his betrothed, who was with child. Now it happened that while they were there, the time came for her to have her child, and she gave birth to a son, her first-born. She wrapped him in swaddling clothes, and laid him in a manger because there was no room for them at the inn.

Luke 2.1–7

4. The Presentation of Jesus in the Temple

And when the day came for them to be purified in keeping with the Law of Moses, they took Jesus up to Jerusalem to present him to the Lord – observing what stands written in the law of the Lord: Every first-born male must be con-secrated to the Lord – and also to offer in sacrifice, in accordance with what is said in the Law of the Lord, a pair of turtledoves or two young pigeons. Now in Jerusalem there was a man named Simeon. He was an upright and devout man; he looked forward to the restoration of Israel and the Holy Spirit rested on him. It had been revealed to him by the Holy Spirit that he would not see death until he had set eyes on the Christ of the Lord. Prompted by the Spirit he came to the Temple: and when the parents brought in the child Jesus to do for him what the Law required, he took him in his arms and blessed God.

As the child's father and mother stood there wondering at the things that were being said about him, Simeon blessed them and said to Mary his mother 'Look, this child is destined for the fall and for the rising of many in Israel, destined to be a sign that is opposed – and a sword will pierce your soul too – so that the secret thoughts of many may be laid bare.'

Luke 2.22–35

5. The finding of the child Jesus in the Temple

Every year his parents used to go to Jerusalem for the feast of the Passover. When he was twelve years old, they went up for the feast as usual. When the days of the feast were over and they set off home, the boy Jesus stayed behind in Jerusalem without his parents knowing it. They assumed he was somewhere in the party, and it was only after a day's journey that they went to look for him among their relations and acquaintances. When they failed to find him they went back to Jerusalem looking for him everywhere.

It happened that, three days later, they found him in the Temple, sitting among the doctors, listening to them, and asking them questions; and all those who heard him were astounded at his intelligence and his replies. They were overcome when they saw him, and his mother said to him, 'My child, why have you done this to us? See how worried your father and I have been, looking for you.' He replied, 'Why were you looking for me? Did you not know that I must be busy in my Father's house?' But they did not understand what he meant.

He went down with them and came to Nazareth and lived under their authority. His mother stored up all these things in her heart. And Jesus increased in wisdom, in stature, and in favour with God and with people.

Luke 2.41–52

The sorrowful mysteries

1.The agony of our blessed Lord in the garden of Gethsemane
He then left to make his way as usual to the Mount of Olives, with the disciples following. When they reached the place he said to them, 'Pray not to be put to the test.'

Then he withdrew from them, about a stone's throw away, and knelt down and prayed. 'Father,' he said, 'if you are willing, take this cup away from me. Nevertheless, let your will be done, not mine.' Then an angel appeared to him, coming from heaven to give him strength. In his anguish he prayed even more earnestly, and his sweat fell to the ground like great drops of blood.

When he rose from prayer he went to the disciples and found them sleeping for sheer grief. And he said to them, 'Why are you asleep? Get up and pray not to be put to the test.'

Suddenly while he was still speaking a number of men appeared, and at the head of them the man called Judas, one of the Twelve, who went up to Jesus to kiss him. Jesus said, 'Judas, are you betraying the Son of Man with a kiss?'

Luke 22.39–48

2.The scourging of our blessed Lord at the pillar
Pilate said to the people, 'What am I to do with Jesus who is called Christ?' They all said, 'Let him be crucified!' He asked, 'But what harm has he done?' But they shouted all the louder, 'Let him be crucified!' Then Pilate saw that he was making no impression, that in fact a riot was imminent. So he took some water, washed his hands in front of the crowd and said, 'I am innocent of this man's blood. It is your concern.' And the people, every one of them, shouted back, 'His blood be on us and on our children!' Then he released Barabbas for them. After having Jesus scourged he then handed him over to be crucified.

Matthew 27.22–26

3. Jesus is crowned with thorns

Pilate then had Jesus taken away and scourged; and after this, the soldiers twisted some thorns into a crown and put it on his head, and dressed him in a purple robe. They kept coming up to him and saying, 'Hail, king of the Jews!' and slapping him in the face.

Pilate came outside again and said to the people, 'Look, I am going to bring him out to you to let you see that I find no case.' Jesus then came out wearing the crown of thorns and the purple robe. Pilate said, 'Here is the man.' When they saw him the chief priests and the guards shouted, 'Crucify him! Crucify him!' Pilate said, 'Take him yourselves and crucify him: I can find no case against him.'

John 19.2–6

4. The carrying of the Cross

They led Jesus out to crucify him. They enlisted a passer-by, Simon of Cyrene, father of Alexander and Rufus, who was coming in from the country, to carry his cross. They brought Jesus to the place called Golgotha, which means the place of the skull.

They offered him wine mixed with myrrh, but he refused it. Then they crucified him, and shared out his clothing, casting lots to decide what each should get. It was the third hour when they crucified him. The inscription giving the charge against him read: The King of the Jews. And they crucified two robbers with him, one on his right and one on his left.

Mark 15.21–27

5. The crucifixion and death of Jesus

Near the cross of Jesus stood his mother and his mother's sister, Mary the wife of Clopas, and Mary of Magdala. Seeing his mother and the disciple whom he loved standing near her, Jesus said to his mother, 'Woman, this is your son.' Then to the disciple he said, 'This is your mother.' And from that hour the disciple took her into his home. After this, Jesus knew that everything had now been completed, and, so that the Scriptures should be completely fulfilled, he said, 'I am thirsty.' A jar full of sour wine stood there, so putting a sponge soaked in the wine on a hyssop stick, they held it up to his mouth. After Jesus had taken the wine he said, 'It is fulfilled;' and bowing his head he gave up his spirit.

John 19.25–30

The glorious mysteries

1.The Resurrection

After the Sabbath, and towards dawn on the first day of the week, Mary
of Magdala and the other Mary went to visit the sepulchre. And suddenly
there was a violent earthquake, for the angel of the Lord, descending
from heaven, came and rolled away the stone and sat on it. His face was
like lightning, his robe white as snow. The guards were so shaken, so
frightened of him, that they were like dead men. But the angel spoke;
and he said to the women, 'There is no need for you to be afraid. I know
you are looking for Jesus, who was crucified. He is not here, for he has
risen, as he said he would. Come and see the place where he lay, then go
quickly and tell his disciples, "He has risen from the dead and now he is
going ahead of you to Galilee; that is where you will see him." Look!
I have told you.' Filled with awe and great joy the women came quickly
away from the tomb and ran to tell his disciples.

Matthew 28.1–8

2.The Ascension

Now having met together, the disciples asked Jesus, 'Lord, has the time
come for you to restore the kingdom to Israel?' He replied, 'It is not
for you to know times or dates that the Father has decided by his own
authority, but you will receive the power of the Holy Spirit which will
come on you, and then you will be my witnesses not only in Jerusalem
but throughout Judaea and Samaria, and indeed to earth's remotest end.'
As he said this he was lifted up while they looked on, and a cloud took
him from their sight.

They were still staring into the sky as he went, when suddenly two
men in white were standing beside them and they said, 'Why are you
Galileans standing here looking into the sky? This Jesus who has been
taken up from you into heaven will come back in the same way as you
have seen him go to heaven.'

Acts 1.6–11

3. The descent of the Holy Spirit on the apostles

When Pentecost day came round, they had all met together, when suddenly there came from heaven a sound as of a violent wind which filled the entire house in which they were sitting; and there appeared to them tongues as of fire; these separated and came to rest on the head of each of them. They were all filled with the Holy Spirit, and began to speak different languages as the Spirit gave them power to express themselves.

And everyone was filled with awe: the apostles worked many signs and miracles. And all who shared the faith owned everything in common; they sold their goods and distributed the proceeds among themselves according to what each one needed.

Each day, with one heart, they regularly went to the Temple but met in their houses for the breaking of bread; they shared their food gladly and generously; they praised God and were looked up to by everyone. Day by day the Lord added to their community those destined to be saved.

Acts 2.1–4; 43–47

4. The Assumption of Our Lady into heaven

Someone may ask, 'How are dead people raised, and what sort of body do they have when they come?' How foolish! What you sow must die before it is given new life and what you sow is not the body that is to be, but only a bare grain, say of wheat or some other kind; it is God who gives it the sort of body that he has chosen for it: and for each kind of seed its own kind of body.

Now I am going to tell you a mystery: we are not all going to fall asleep, but we are all going to be changed, instantly, in the twinkling of an eye, when the last trumpet sounds. The trumpet is going to sound, and then the dead will be raised imperishable, and we shall be changed, because this perishable nature of ours must put on imperishability, this mortal nature must put on immortality. And after this perishable nature has put on imperishability, and this mortal nature has put on immortality, then will the words of Scripture come true:

> 'Death is swallowed up in victory.
> Death, where is your victory?
> Death, where is your sting?'

The sting of death is sin, and the power of sin comes from the Law. Thank God, then, for giving us the victory through Jesus Christ our Lord.

1 Corinthians 15.35–37; 51–57

5. The Coronation of Our Lady in heaven and the glory of the saints

After that I saw that there was a huge number, impossible for anyone to count, of people from every nation, race, tribe and language; they were standing in front of the throne and in front of the Lamb, dressed in white robes and holding palms in their hands. They shouted in a loud voice: 'Salvation to our God, who sits on the throne and to the Lamb!' And all the angels who were standing in a circle round the throne, surrounding the elders and the four living creatures, prostrated themselves before the throne and touched the ground with their foreheads, worshipping God with these words:

'Amen. Praise and glory and wisdom and thanksgiving
and honour and power and strength
to our God for ever and ever. Amen.'

One of the elders then spoke, and asked me, 'Who are these people, dressed in white robes, and where have they come from?' I answered him, 'You can tell me, sir'. Then he said, 'These are the people who have been through the great trial, they have washed their robes white again in the blood of the Lamb. That is why they are now standing in front of God's throne and serving him day and night in his sanctuary; and the One who sits on the throne will spread his tent over them. They will never hunger or thirst again; sun and scorching wind will never plague them, because the Lamb who is at the heart of the throne will be their shepherd and will guide them to springs of living water, and God will wipe away all tears from their eyes.'

Revelation 7.9–17

At the conclusion of the Rosary the following prayers are said:

Hail, holy queen, mother of mercy; hail, our life, our sweetness and our hope. To you do we cry, poor banished children of Eve; to you do we send up our sighs, mourning and weeping in this vale of tears. Turn then, most gracious advocate, your eyes of mercy towards us; and after this our exile, show unto us the blessed fruit of your womb, Jesus. O clement, O loving, O sweet Virgin Mary.

> V. Pray for us, holy Mother of God:
> R. That we may be made worthy of the promises of Christ.

O God, whose only-begotten Son, by his life, death and resurrection, has purchased for us the rewards of eternal life: grant that meditating on these mysteries in the most holy Rosary of the Blessed Virgin Mary, we may both imitate what they contain, and obtain what they promise; through the same Christ our Lord.

Prayer for England

In the Middle Ages England was known as Our Lady's Dowry, because there were more churches dedicated to Mary than to any other title. This prayer, in its original form written by Cardinal Merry del Val, has traditionally been said at Benediction. It is a prayer for the unity of the Church in our country.

O Blessed Virgin Mary, Mother of God, and our most gentle queen and mother, look down in mercy upon England, your dowry, and upon us all who greatly hope and trust in you. By you it was that Jesus, our Saviour and our hope, was given to the world; and he has given you to us that we may hope still more.

Plead for us your children, whom you received and accepted at the foot of the cross, O mother of sorrows. Pray for our separated brethren, that in the one true fold of Christ, we may all be united under the care of Pope _____, the chief shepherd of Christ's flock. Pray for us all, dear mother, that, by faith and fruitful in good works, we may all deserve to see and praise God, together with you in our heavenly home.

IX: Other Devotions

The Stations of the Cross

From early times Christians began to go to Jerusalem in order to visit
the holy places associated with the death of Jesus, and to follow the
footsteps of his last journey to the Cross. Not much later they began
to build churches in their home towns to remind them of the Holy
Land. Inside a church it became common to mark the different stages
or 'stations' of the Way of the Cross. Some of these did not belong to
the story we find in the Gospels but to popular legend which had
become part of the traditional devotion. The Stations of the Cross
help us enter into the Passion story for ourselves. They are a way of
meditating on the suffering of Jesus and its relevance to our own
world and our lives in it. We can focus our attention on Jesus, on the
other people who enter into the story, and on ourselves. When we
walk the Way of the Cross we are at the side of Jesus, stopping at each
station to fill our minds with the thought of his suffering, but we also
think of the faith and love he showed right to the moment of his
death. We pray with sorrow for our sins; and we remember that the
evil which led to the death of Jesus is still the cause of innocent
suffering today. In the battle against evil, the struggle continues and
we have our part to play alongside Jesus. Yet we fight in the firm hope
of Jesus' victory over sin and death. We know that the seal of Jesus'
tomb was to break open on the third day, and open up the way to
new life and glory in the resurrection.

Opening prayer

Jesus Christ, my Lord, with what great love you passed over the painful road which led you to death; and I, how often have I abandoned you. But now I love you with my whole soul, and because I love you, I am sincerely sorry for having offended you. My Jesus, pardon me, and permit me to accompany you in this journey. You are going to die for love of me, and it is my wish also, my dearest redeemer, to die for love of you. Jesus, in your love I wish to live, in your love I wish to die.

At each station

> V. We adore you, O Christ, and we praise you:
> R. Because by your holy Cross you have redeemed the world.

Reflection

Act of Contrition

> I love you Jesus, my love, above all things; I repent with my whole heart for having offended you. Never permit me to separate myself from you again. Grant that I may love you always, then do with me what you will.

Then it is customary to say:

> Our Father . . . Hail Mary . . . Glory be . . .

Jesus is condemned to death   First Station

Jesus stands before Pilate. His followers have betrayed him and run away. He has been rejected by his people, insulted, crowned with thorns and unjustly condemned. Even Pilate who has sentenced him to death, either cynically or fearfully, would like to wash his hands of the matter, and yet seems fascinated by Jesus, who he is, how he is able to live even the end of his life so peacefully. Standing opposite each other are two powers, two attitudes to life.

We are reminded how easy it is to pass judgement unjustly, without knowledge of the truth or understanding of another person; how easy to echo the prejudices of those who shout loudest or whom we need to please. And we are reminded of our own feelings when we stand wrongly accused, when people are not listening to the truth of what we are trying to say.

Jesus receives the cross   Second Station

The beam of the Cross is laid on Jesus' back which has already been
wounded by beating. In receiving it Jesus is not just a passive victim.
He accepts what he knows now to be the will of his Father; his whole
life of obedience has led to this and he trusts in the Father's strength to
persevere to the end. For by loving us to the end, Jesus wants to save
the world.

What is our cross? Our failings, our weakness, our fears? Our
responsibility for others brings a burden we sometimes feel we do
not have the strength to support. And yet Jesus tells his disciples to take
up their cross every day: that is how we follow his path to life, a life
for others as well as for ourselves. He has already felt the weight and
supports us as we follow him. 'Take my yoke upon you and learn from
me, for I am gentle and humble in heart.'

Jesus falls the first time   Third Station

But at the very outset of the journey he falls to the ground. Even Jesus'
physical strength is not enough to match his desire to save us. Yet the
power of God is made perfect in weakness.

This station reminds us how easily we fall because of our weakness
and human limitations. It asks us to think about how tiredness and
suffering affects our readiness to follow Christ, how quickly we are
discouraged, or get lazy. How ready are we to ask for help from God,
to draw on the strength of the Holy Spirit rather than trust in our own
strength? Jesus fell too, not from sin but because he shared our weakness.
He only asks us to let him pick us up and forgive us our sins.

Jesus is met by his blessed mother   Fourth Station

At this point in popular legend, Jesus meets his mother Mary. It will have been a painful moment for them both; such is the bond between a child and his mother, and the hopes that any parent has for a child. She had followed him from Galilee, watching and trying to understand. Simeon had prophesied when she brought the new-born Jesus to the Temple that a sword would pierce her heart because of her son. Now she must begin again to understand the mystery of her son's life in a new light.

Shining through the anguish of this scene, however, is the mother's constancy, her desire to be with her son, whatever happens, however little she understands. The bond of faith uniting mother and son is stronger than all the pain. This compassion gives Mary a special place in the mystery of our salvation. As the Old Testament poem in the Song of Songs says: 'Many waters cannot quench love, neither can the floods drown it. Love is strong as death.'

Simon of Cyrene helps Jesus carry his cross   Fifth Station

The Gospels tell us that, as Jesus staggered under the burden of the cross, the soldiers forced a visitor to Jerusalem to help. We do not know why he was in the crowd, what his feelings were about Jesus. Perhaps it was easy for the soldiers to pick on him, a foreigner, dragging him in to share the mockery of Jesus by the people. The tradition, however, was that the experience turned his heart and his act of obedience made him one of the first to believe.

This scene makes us think of our own irritability when circumstances force us to act when we prefer a quiet life and not to get involved, especially when it means unpopularity or scorn. At these times we need to pray for courage to do what we see is right and good. But this scene also teaches us that the efforts and sacrifices we make, even reluctantly, have a part to play in God's work of salvation, and can become for us a source of grace.

Veronica wipes the face of Jesus   Sixth Station

Veronica is drawn into the story of the Passion like Simon, but in her case voluntarily. In the legend of the Way of the Cross, her attention was caught by Jesus. Behind the blood and sweat, and the popular abuse, she saw a human being, whose suffering called forth her human pity. A simple gesture, in itself of little consequence, to wipe Jesus' face with her clothes. And yet the precious thing here is the simplicity of the human gesture, and of the heart which prompted it. The woman's name was remembered as Veronica from the Latin vera icon (true image) because the legend was that the woman's veil was marked with a true image of Jesus.

We pray that, like Veronica, we will be able to see Jesus' face in other people, especially those in need, and be able to see them not as a problem but as individuals with a claim on our attention. In our response, we also pray we will have something of her simplicity of heart. For she teaches us that even the smallest human gestures can be a way of showing other people something of what Jesus looks like.

Jesus falls the second time   Seventh Station

After three scenes where Jesus' suffering is met in different ways by Mary, Simon and Veronica, we are back in the crowd watching him fall a second time. This time there is no one to help, no sympathy.

What is our response to Jesus? We are reminded of the loneliness that pain causes someone who is suffering it, be the pain physical or mental. We are reminded of how slow we are to respond, how easily we overlook other people's isolation, and stand back in the crowd. It is because of our own sinfulness that Jesus falls, and yet it is his patience and perseverance that can give us hope and courage to be generous in doing good.

The women of Jerusalem   Eighth Station

Even in the crowd are those who feel sorry about what was happening.
They even have the courage to speak out, if not in protest, at least with
regret. Jesus' reply is a warning: 'Weep not for me, but for yourselves
and your children.'

It is no good feeling sorrow for what Jesus undergoes unless we are
ready to do something about it. For we are the cause of his suffering.
Only a change of heart will let us see the Passion in its proper
perspective; Jesus wants us to recognize our responsibility for human
suffering and for putting to right the wrongs of the world.

Jesus falls for the third time   Ninth Station

As he reaches the top of Golgotha where he was crucified, according to
the traditional devotion, Jesus collapses for a third and last time. In terms
of his human strength, Jesus has reached rock bottom; the rest of the way
he is driven on simply by the determination of others to finish him off.
Helpless as he is, Jesus is still the obedient Son of his heavenly Father,
who 'for the prize of our salvation that was set before him' did not refuse
his cross, but held fast to hope.

It is our Lord's tenacity to the end which can encourage us to be
faithful when we find our weakness letting us down, and we fall again
and again into habits of sin.

It is too easy to let the routine of life lead us to compromise our
moral and spiritual integrity as human beings and to give up on the
ideals with which we set out so hopefully. May the figure of Jesus on the
ground of Golgotha teach us never to let our hearts become hard or cold.

Jesus is stripped of his garments   Tenth Station

The public humiliation of a criminal continues. Just as Jesus had stripped
himself of his glory as God in order to save us, so now his own clothes are
stripped off and his dignity as a human being is vilified. Not only
outwardly, but also in his heart Jesus has been stripped of everything
he could call his own, except his obedience to the will of his Father and
the core faith, hope and love which animated his will to see it through.

As we think of this scene we can learn what Jesus meant when he
said 'Blessed are the poor in spirit, for theirs is the Kingdom of heaven;
blessed are the pure in heart, for they shall see God.' We can only be
amazed at our own concern for trivialities, and the pettiness of so much
of our human ambition.

Jesus is nailed to the Cross   Eleventh Station

Cruelty and barbarism are not just features of the Roman world; the
modern world has found many ways of dehumanizing other people
thoughtlessly in the name of greed and selfishness. Jesus did not refuse to
be identified with the most vilified outcast of society. And yet in making
himself the victim of our injustice and insensitivity to others Jesus has
opened up a new way for us to find our true humanity. He stretches out
his arms to embrace the world in his love, regardless of the excruciating
pain and the loss of his lifeblood. He does not condemn the world but
touches our hearts so that we may turn to him in sorrow and repentance
and be saved. 'Forgive us our sins as we forgive those who sin against us.'

Jesus dies on the Cross   Twelfth station

Jesus hung for three hours in the heat of the day, enduring the agony
of pain and thirst, as he struggled for breath against the downward pull
of his body from the arms of the cross. Each movement up or down
increased the cutting of the nails through his hands and feet. At the same
time, according to the Gospel story, he forgave his murderers, entrusted
his mother Mary and John, the beloved disciple, to each other's care, and
he promised heaven to the repentant thief. Now he knows that he has
finished his life's work, and can surrender everything to his Father putting
himself into his hands. 'Greater love has no one than this,' he had said,
'than to lay down his life for his friends.'

Jesus is taken down from the Cross   Thirteenth Station

After Jesus' death, his mother, together with others among the women disciples, Joseph of Arimathea and Nicodemus, obtained permission to take the dead body down from the Cross and bury it in a tomb nearby. Finally in the quiet of the evening, the crowds departed, they are able to mourn the one they have lost, in whom, during his life, they had seen so much.

On the one hand this is a picture of human tenderness and feeling, caring for a body, so brutally treated, now lifeless and empty. On the other hand we still hear echoing the words of the Roman centurion who was on duty at the end of that day: 'Truly this was the Son of God.' Even though he is dead it is possible to turn to Jesus in faith. It is with that faith in the death of Jesus that we try to face the mystery of death which will meet us all.

Jesus is placed in the tomb   Fourteenth Station

The tomb is sealed so that Jesus may make even the grave a milestone on our road to glory with him. This is where the Way of the Cross traditionally ends. Yet the end of Jesus' life is only the beginning of the story of his life in our hearts. 'We must suffer in faith, wait in hope and rise above everything in love.'

> I know that my redeemer lives, and on the last day, he will stand on the earth and, after my skin has been destroyed, from my flesh I shall see God, whom I shall see on my side, and my eyes shall behold him and no other.

Job 19.25–27

Final Prayer

> V. Christ was made for us obedient unto death:
> R. Even death on a cross.

Look down, O Lord, upon this your family, for which our Lord Jesus Christ did not refuse to be delivered into the hands of the wicked and to endure the torments of the Cross; who lives and reigns with you in the unity of the Holy Spirit, one God, for ever and ever.

Prayers and Hymns to the Holy Spirit

Prayers for the guidance of the Holy Spirit

Come Holy Spirit, fill the hearts of your faithful, and kindle in them the fire of your love.

> V. Send forth your Spirit and they shall be created:
> R. And you shall renew the face of the earth.

Let us pray:
O God, who taught the hearts of your faithful by the light of the Holy Spirit, grant that by the gift of the same Spirit we may be always truly wise and ever rejoice in his consolation; through Christ our Lord.

O Lord, you have taught us that all our actions are worth nothing without charity; send your Holy Spirit upon us and pour into our hearts that most excellent gift of charity, the very bond of peace and of all virtues, without which whoever lives is counted dead before you; through Jesus Christ our Lord.

The Book of Common Prayer

Set our hearts on fire with love of you, O Christ our God, that in its flame we may love you with all our heart, with all our mind, with all our soul and with all our strength, and our neighbours as ourselves, so that, keeping your commandments, we may glorify your name.

Orthodox prayer

Holy Spirit, be with us throughout this day.
Strengthen us in our work, enlighten us in our study,
make us constantly aware of each other and of you,
so that we may live every moment of this day as you would have us do.

Michael Buckley

Veni Sancte Spiritus

Come thou Holy Paraclete,
And from thy celestial seat
Send thy light and brilliancy.
Father of the poor, draw near;
Giver of all gifts be here;
Come, the soul's true radiancy.

Thou of comforters the best,
Thou the soul's most welcome guest,
Come in toil refreshingly.
In our labour rest most sweet,
Thou art coolness in the heat,
Comfort in adversity.

O most blessed Light divine,
Shine within these hearts of thine,
And our inmost being fill;
Where thou art not, man hath naught,
Nothing good in deed or thought,
Nothing free from taint of ill.

Heal our wounds; our strength renew;
On our dryness pour thy dew;
Wash the stains of guilt away;
Bend the stubborn heart and will;
Melt the frozen, warm the chill;
Guide the steps that go astray.

On the faithful who adore
And confess thee, evermore
In thy sevenfold gifts descend:
Give them virtue's sure reward,
Give them thy salvation, Lord,
Give them joys that never end.

Veni Creator Spiritus

Creating Spirit, come possess
Our souls, and with thy presence bless;
And in our hearts framed by thy hand,
Let thy celestial grace command.

Thou who art called the Paraclete,
The almighty Father's gift complete;
The living fountain, fire and love
With grace anointing from above;

Thou finger of the Father's hand,
Who dost a sevenfold gift command;
True promise from the Highest sent,
In different tongues now eloquent.

Cleanse with thy light our sinful parts
And with thy love inflame our hearts;
Our human weakness fortify
With everlasting constancy.

Far from us drive our deadly foe,
And peace the fruit of love bestow;
Thus having thee our safest guide,
Let not our feet to evil slide.

Let us by thee the Father own,
And to us let his Son be known
Let us believe in thee who dost
From both proceed, the Holy Ghost.

To God the Father and the Son
Who rose from death, be homage done;
May we always our praise repeat
To God the Holy Paraclete.

Prayers to the Saints

Patron saints of the British Isles

St David (1 March)
Almighty God, may the prayers of St David, your monk and bishop, protect us, so that as we celebrate his life and work in Wales we may be, like him, strenuous defenders of the Christian faith; through Jesus Christ our Lord.

St Patrick (17 March)
We thank you, almighty God, for sending St Patrick to preach the Gospel to the people of Ireland. May we who share his faith imitate his example and bring the good news of salvation to all with whom we live and work; through Jesus Christ our Lord.

St George (23 April)
Almighty God, you blessed St George with a spirit of bravery to follow Christ in his suffering and death; by his prayers may your blessing be upon England; and grant us, like him, a spirit of gentleness and courtesy in our Christian life; through Jesus Christ our Lord.

St Andrew (30 November)
Lord God, you called St Andrew to follow you, to preach the Gospel and to lead the Church as an apostle. We pray that as our faith is built on the foundation of the apostles, so may we grow through our fellowship with them into true witnesses of your Son, Jesus Christ, and share with them the fulness of new life; through the same Jesus Christ our Lord.

Other saints

St Augustine of Canterbury
Father, you sent St Augustine to preach the Gospel to the people of
England. May the work he began be renewed in this land and continue
to prosper. Grant this through our Lord Jesus Christ your Son, who lives
and reigns with you and the Holy Spirit, one God for ever and ever.

St Benedict
Father, you called Saint Benedict to leave everything to follow you and
made him a master in the school of your service: inspired by his life
and teaching may our hearts expand with love so that prompted by the
Gospel we may run with him along the path of true life; through Jesus
Christ our Lord.

Stir up in your Church, O Lord, that Spirit to which our Holy Father
St Benedict was obedient, that filled with the same Spirit we may strive
to love what he loved and put into practice what he taught; through
Jesus Christ our Lord.

Grant unto us, we beseech you, O Lord, a persevering service in your
will, that in our day, both in merit and in number, the people who serve
you may be increased; through Jesus Christ our Lord.

St Gregory
Father, you inspired Saint Gregory to send monks as teachers of the
Gospel in this land and to strengthen our communion with the whole
Church. Bless all our pastors and teachers of the faith that the Church in
England may continue to grow in love of you and in its service of the
Gospel; through Jesus Christ our Lord.

May the prayers of Saint Gregory help us to live more faithfully. As he
preferred the honour of being the servant of the servants of God to that
of earthly power, may we be as generous as he was in living our lives to
bring others the knowledge of your compassionate love; through Jesus
Christ our Lord.

English Martyrs

Heavenly Father, we thank you for the men and women who gave their lives for the integrity of the Catholic faith in this land: may we be united with them in our faith and worship, and strive with them for the unity of the Church for which they longed, according to the mind of your only Son, our Saviour, Jesus Christ.

An Irish Martyr – St Oliver Plunkett (1 July)

God our Father, you filled St Oliver with the courage to be a good shepherd and lay down his life for your sheep. Help us by his prayers to keep the faith he taught and follow the way of reconciliation which he showed by his example.

For any Saint

O God, you have brought us near to an innumerable company of angels and to the spirits of the just made perfect; grant us on our pilgrimage to abide in their fellowship, and in our heavenly country be united with their joy; through Christ our Lord.

William Bright

Almighty father, through your grace the saints reflect your holiness in many different ways: grant that we may be encouraged by their example and supported by their prayers, and so reach the heights of virtue to which you have called us

Blessed are all your saints, O God and King, who have travelled over the tempestuous sea of this life and have reached at last the harbour of peace. Watch over us who are still on voyage. Frail is our vessel and the ocean is wide, but as you have set our course, so steer the vessel of our life towards the everlasting shore of peace, and bring us at last to the quiet haven of our heart's desire; through Jesus Christ our Lord.

St Augustine

Litanies

Prayer is always an expression of faith. A litany is a simple way of praying which combines a meditation on part of our faith in God and his salvation with an appeal to his love and mercy. A litany is a repetitive form of prayer and, as with the Rosary, the point of repetition is to deepen the level of our prayer, so that it comes more from the heart than the mind. It is meditative prayer, which uses simple truths of our faith to keep the mind turned towards God while we pray increasingly from the heart. No meditative prayer will work if we try to do it quickly or unthinkingly, but we do not need to think much, just keep our minds on the job.

These five litanies – of the Sacred Heart, Holy Name of Jesus, the Holy Spirit, Our Lady, and the Saints – begin by turning to God, Father, Son and Spirit, for mercy. The Lord have Mercy or Kyrie Eleison at Mass is itself a remnant of a much longer litany, introduced many centuries ago as a hymn of worship to the Trinity. Repeatedly calling on God's mercy lets us be absorbed by the scale of his love which he shows in all his actions towards us. Each of the litanies develops a series of ideas connected to an aspect of our faith which constantly brings us back to the adoration of God's merciful love.

Litany of the Sacred Heart

Lord, have mercy:	Lord, have mercy
Christ, have mercy:	Christ, have mercy
Lord, have mercy:	Lord, have mercy
Christ, hear us:	Christ, graciously hear us

God, the Father of heaven,	have mercy on us
God, the Son, redeemer of the world,	have mercy on us
God, the Holy Spirit,	have mercy on us
Holy Trinity, one God,	have mercy on us

Heart of Jesus, Son of the eternal Father,	have mercy on us
Heart of Jesus, formed by the Holy Spirit in the womb of the Virgin Mother,	have mercy on us
Heart of Jesus, wonderfully united to the eternal Word,	have mercy on us
Heart of Jesus, of infinite majesty,	have mercy on us
Heart of Jesus, holy temple of God,	have mercy on us
Heart of Jesus, tabernacle of the Most High,	have mercy on us
Heart of Jesus, house of God and gate of heaven,	have mercy on us
Heart of Jesus, burning furnace of charity,	have mercy on us
Heart of Jesus, vessel of justice and love,	have mercy on us
Heart of Jesus, never-ending source of all virtues,	have mercy on us
Heart of Jesus, worthy of all praise,	have mercy on us
Heart of Jesus, king and centre of all hearts,	have mercy on us
Heart of Jesus, in which are all the treasures of wisdom and knowledge,	have mercy on us
Heart of Jesus, in which dwells all the fullness of the divinity,	have mercy on us
Heart of Jesus, in which the Father is well pleased,	have mercy on us
Heart of Jesus, of whose fullness we have all received,	have mercy on us
Heart of Jesus, deepest desire of the human heart,	have mercy on us
Heart of Jesus, patient and abounding in mercy,	have mercy on us
Heart of Jesus, generous to all who call upon you,	have mercy on us
Heart of Jesus, fountain of life and holiness,	have mercy on us
Heart of Jesus, atonement for our sins,	have mercy on us
Heart of Jesus, which suffered rejection for our sake,	have mercy on us
Heart of Jesus, bruised for our sins,	have mercy on us
Heart of Jesus, made obedient unto death,	have mercy on us
Heart of Jesus, pierced with a lance,	have mercy on us

Heart of Jesus, source of all consolation,	have mercy on us
Heart of Jesus, our peace and reconciliation,	have mercy on us
Heart of Jesus, victim of our sins,	have mercy on us
Heart of Jesus, salvation of those who hope in you,	have mercy on us
Heart of Jesus, hope of those who die in you,	have mercy on us
Heart of Jesus, our light and resurrection,	have mercy on us
Heart of Jesus, delight of all the saints,	have mercy on us
Lamb of God, you take away the sins of the world,	spare us, O Lord
Lamb of God, you take away the sins of the world,	graciously hear us, O Lord
Lamb of God, you take away the sins of the world,	have mercy on us
Jesus, meek and humble of heart:	make our hearts like unto your heart

Almighty and eternal God, look upon the heart of your beloved Son
and the praises and sacrifice he offers you in the name of sinners; being
pleased with his holy obedience, pardon those who seek your mercy
and grant us a share in his resurrection; through the same Jesus Christ
your Son who lives and reigns with you in the unity of the Holy Spirit,
world without end.

Litany of the Most Holy Name of Jesus

The Jesus Prayer is one of the most ancient prayers of the Church
meditating on Jesus. His name means 'God saves', and this prayer
does no more than repeat the name with an acclamation of faith
in his identity as the Son of God. The prayer exists in several
forms. The easiest to use is: *Lord Jesus Christ, Son of God, have mercy on us*.
The Litany of the Name of Jesus explores the meaning of Jesus'
life more systematically as an extended prayer of adoration.

Lord, have mercy:	Lord, have mercy
Christ, have mercy:	Christ, have mercy
Lord, have mercy:	Lord, have mercy
Jesus, hear us:	Jesus, graciously hear us

God, the Father of heaven,	have mercy on us
God, the Son, redeemer of the world,	have mercy on us
God, the Holy Spirit,	have mercy on us
Holy Trinity, one God,	have mercy on us
Jesus, Son of the living God,	have mercy on us
Jesus, splendour of the Father,	have mercy on us
Jesus, brightness of eternal light,	have mercy on us
Jesus, king of glory,	have mercy on us
Jesus, sun of justice,	have mercy on us
Jesus, born of the Virgin Mary,	have mercy on us
Jesus, most amiable,	have mercy on us
Jesus, most admirable,	have mercy on us
Jesus, mighty God,	have mercy on us
Jesus, father of the world to come,	have mercy on us
Jesus, angel of great counsel,	have mercy on us
Jesus, most powerful,	have mercy on us
Jesus, most patient,	have mercy on us
Jesus, most obedient,	have mercy on us
Jesus, meek and humble of heart,	have mercy on us
Jesus, lover of purity,	have mercy on us
Jesus, lover of us,	have mercy on us
Jesus, author of life,	have mercy on us
Jesus, perfection of all virtues,	have mercy on us
Jesus, zealous lover of souls,	have mercy on us
Jesus, our refuge,	have mercy on us
Jesus, father of the poor,	have mercy on us
Jesus, treasure of the faithful,	have mercy on us
Jesus, good shepherd,	have mercy on us
Jesus, true light,	have mercy on us
Jesus, eternal wisdom,	have mercy on us
Jesus, infinite goodness,	have mercy on us
Jesus, our way and our life,	have mercy on us

Jesus, joy of angels,	have mercy on us
Jesus, king of patriarchs,	have mercy on us
Jesus, master of the apostles,	have mercy on us
Jesus, teacher of the evangelists,	have mercy on us
Jesus, strength of martyrs,	have mercy on us
Jesus, light of confessors,	have mercy on us
Jesus, purity of virgins,	have mercy on us
Jesus, crown of all the saints,	have mercy on us
Be merciful unto us,	Jesus, spare us
From all evil,	Jesus, deliver us
From all sin,	Jesus, deliver us
From all wrath,	Jesus, deliver us
From the snares of the devil,	Jesus, deliver us
From everlasting death,	Jesus, deliver us
From our failure to follow your inspiration,	Jesus, deliver us
Through the mystery of your holy incarnation,	Jesus, deliver us
Through your nativity,	Jesus, deliver us
Through your infancy,	Jesus, deliver us
Through your most divine life,	Jesus, deliver us
Through your labours,	Jesus, deliver us
Through your agony and passion,	Jesus, deliver us
Through your cross and abandonment,	Jesus, deliver us
Through your death and burial,	Jesus, deliver us
Through your resurrection,	Jesus, deliver us
Through your ascension,	Jesus, deliver us
Through your reign in heaven,	Jesus, deliver us
Through your joys,	Jesus, deliver us
Through your glory,	Jesus, deliver us
Lamb of God, you take away the sins of the world,	spare us, O Jesus
Lamb of God, you take away the sins of the world,	graciously hear us, O Jesus
Lamb of God, you take away the sins of the world,	Jesus, graciously hear us.

Lord Jesus Christ, you said: ask and you shall receive; seek and you shall find, knock and it shall be opened unto you. Mercifully listen to our prayers: may we always love you with our whole heart and never cease from praising and glorifying your Holy Name. Give us, Lord, a perpetual love of your holy name; for you never cease to be with those whom you honour in your love, who live and reign world without end.

Litany of the Holy Spirit

The litany of the Holy Spirit brings together the passages of Scripture on which the doctrine of the Holy Spirit is based; in particular, the gifts of the Holy Spirit from Isaiah, and the fruits of the Holy Spirit from St Paul's letter to the Galatians. The part the Spirit played in creation and in the birth and mission of Jesus is one he plays in the life of all who believe.

Lord, have mercy:	Lord, have mercy
Christ, have mercy:	Christ, have mercy
Lord, have mercy:	Lord, have mercy
Christ, hear us:	Christ, graciously hear us
God, the Father of heaven,	have mercy on us
God, the Son, redeemer of the world,	have mercy on us
God, the Holy Spirit,	have mercy on us
Holy Trinity, one God,	have mercy on us
Holy Spirit, proceeding from the Father, and the Son, equal with them in glory and majesty,	have mercy on us
Promise of the Father and gift of the Most High,	have mercy on us
Consuming Fire,	have mercy on us
Spiritual Anointing,	have mercy on us
Spirit of wisdom and understanding,	have mercy on us
Spirit of counsel and strength,	have mercy on us
Spirit of knowledge and godliness,	have mercy on us
Spirit of the fear of the Lord,	have mercy on us

Spirit of grace and holiness,	have mercy on us
Spirit of love, joy and peace,	have mercy on us
Spirit of long-suffering, gentleness and goodness,	have mercy on us
Spirit of truth, meekness and patience,	have mercy on us
Spirit of modesty, temperance and chastity,	have mercy on us
Spirit of compunction and prayer,	have mercy on us
Spirit of faith, hope and love,	have mercy on us
Spirit of peace and unity,	have mercy on us
Holy Spirit, the Comforter,	have mercy on us
Holy Spirit, the sanctifier,	have mercy on us
Holy Spirit, making us children of God,	have mercy on us
Be merciful to us,	Holy Spirit of God
Be merciful to us and hear us,	Holy Spirit of God
From all sin,	deliver us, Holy Spirit of God
From all assaults of the evil one,	deliver us, Holy Spirit of God
From lack of faith,	deliver us, Holy Spirit of God
From weakness of will and despair,	deliver us, Holy Spirit of God
From impatience and hardness of heart,	deliver us, Holy Spirit of God
From lack of self-control and unchastity,	deliver us, Holy Spirit of God
From final impenitence,	deliver us, Holy Spirit of God
By your eternal procession from the Father and the Son,	deliver us, Holy Spirit of God
By your working in creation,	deliver us, Holy Spirit of God
By your inspiration of the prophets,	deliver us, Holy Spirit of God
By your descent on the Virgin Mary at the incarnation,	deliver us, Holy Spirit of God
By your descent on Jesus at his Baptism,	deliver us, Holy Spirit of God
By your descent on Mary and the apostles at Pentecost,	deliver us, Holy Spirit of God
By your continual dwelling in the Church,	deliver us, Holy Spirit of God
By your wonderful power and love,	deliver us, Holy Spirit of God

We, sinners, beseech you to hear us,	Lord, graciously hear us
That you may shed your light and love abroad in our hearts,	Lord, graciously hear us
That you may continue to open up for us the treasures of your grace,	Lord, graciously hear us
That you may teach us to make requests in accordance with your will,	Lord, graciously hear us
That you may teach us to pray, and yourself pray in us,	Lord, graciously hear us
That we may never grieve you by indifference or sin,	Lord, graciously hear us
That we may remember our bodies are temples for your indwelling,	Lord, graciously hear us
That we may follow you as our guide into all truth,	Lord, graciously hear us
That the whole Church may be united by you in love and peace,	Lord, graciously hear us
Lamb of God, you take away the sins of the world,	pour out on us the Holy Spirit
Lamb of God, you take away the sins of the world,	send down on us the Spirit of the Father
Lamb of God, you take away the sins of the world,	grant us the Spirit of peace

Send forth your Spirit O Lord:
And you will renew the face of the earth.

Grant, O merciful Father, that your Holy Spirit may enlighten, inflame and
purify our hearts; that he may shed on us the dew of holiness and make us
fruitful in good works; through Jesus Christ our Lord.

Litany of Our Lady

Known as the Litany of Loreto, the origins of this litany are ancient and reflect the strength of devotion to Mary among Greek-speaking Christians of the early centuries. Several images taken from the Old Testament are used here to describe the uniqueness of her place in the history of salvation. But most significant is the repeated use of the titles of Virgin and Mother as well as her title as Queen of heaven.

Lord, have mercy:	Lord, have mercy
Christ, have mercy:	Christ, have mercy
Lord, have mercy:	Lord, have mercy
Christ, hear us:	Christ, graciously hear us
God the Father of heaven,	have mercy on us
God the Son, redeemer of the world,	have mercy on us
God the Holy Spirit,	have mercy on us
Holy Trinity, one God,	have mercy on us
Holy Mary,	pray for us
Holy Mother of God,	pray for us
Holy Virgin of virgins,	pray for us
Mother of Christ,	pray for us
Mother of the Church,	pray for us
Mother of divine grace,	pray for us
Mother most pure,	pray for us
Mother most chaste,	pray for us
Mother inviolate,	pray for us
Mother undefiled,	pray for us
Mother most lovable,	pray for us
Mother most admirable,	pray for us
Mother of good counsel,	pray for us
Mother of our creator,	pray for us
Mother of our Saviour,	pray for us
Mother most prudent,	pray for us
Mother most venerable,	pray for us
Mother most renowned,	pray for us
Mother most powerful,	pray for us
Mother most merciful,	pray for us

Mother most faithful,	pray for us
Mirror of justice,	pray for us
Cause of our joy,	pray for us
Spiritual vessel,	pray for us
Vessel of honour,	pray for us
Spiritual vessel of devotion,	pray for us
Mystical rose,	pray for us
Tower of David,	pray for us
Tower of ivory,	pray for us
House of gold,	pray for us
Ark of the covenant,	pray for us
Gate of heaven,	pray for us
Morning star,	pray for us
Health of the sick,	pray for us
Refuge of sinners,	pray for us
Comfort of the afflicted,	pray for us
Help of Christians,	pray for us
Queen of angels,	pray for us
Queen of patriarchs,	pray for us
Queen of prophets,	pray for us
Queen of apostles,	pray for us
Queen of martyrs,	pray for us
Queen of confessors,	pray for us
Queen of virgins,	pray for us
Queen of all the saints,	pray for us
Queen conceived without original sin,	pray for us
Queen assumed into heaven,	pray for us
Queen of the most holy Rosary,	pray for us
Queen of families,	pray for us
Queen of peace,	pray for us
Lamb of God, you take away the sins of the world,	spare us, O Lord
Lamb of God, you take away the sins of the world,	graciously hear us, O Lord
Lamb of God, you take away the sins of the world,	have mercy on us

Pray for us, O holy Mother of God:
That we may be made worthy of the promises of Christ.

Grant that we your servants, Lord, may enjoy unfailing health of mind and body, and through the prayers of the Blessed Virgin Mary in her glory, free us from our sorrows in this world and give us eternal happiness with you; through Jesus Christ our Lord.

Litany of the Saints

This litany is the most commonly used in the Church's liturgy. It is used in the Rite of Initiation, at ordinations to the priesthood and episcopal ordination, and also at monastic profession. It is normally adapted to include saints who are particularly close to the person being ordained or professed, either as patrons or examples. We should feel free to follow this practice ourselves and include those saints whose lives are inspirations for our faith and love. The list is organized in various groups as indicated at the end of each section.

Lord, have mercy:	Lord, have mercy
Christ, have mercy:	Christ, have mercy
Lord, have mercy:	Lord, have mercy
Christ, hear us:	Christ, graciously hear us
God the Father of heaven,	have mercy on us
God the Son, redeemer of the world,	have mercy on us
God the Holy Spirit,	have mercy on us
Holy Trinity, one God,	have mercy on us
Holy Mary,	pray for us
Holy Mother of God,	pray for us
Holy Virgin of virgins,	pray for us
St Michael,	pray for us
St Gabriel,	pray for us
St Raphael,	pray for us
All holy angels and archangels,	pray for us

St John the Baptist,	pray for us
St Joseph,	pray for us
All holy patriarchs and prophets,	pray for us
St Peter,	pray for us
St Paul,	pray for us
St Andrew,	pray for us
St John,	pray for us
St James,	pray for us
St Philip,	pray for us
St Bartholomew,	pray for us
St Matthew,	pray for us
St Simon,	pray for us
St Thaddeus,	pray for us
St Matthias,	pray for us
St Barnabas,	pray for us
St Luke,	pray for us
St Mark,	pray for us
All holy apostles and evangelists,	pray for us
All holy disciples of our Lord,	pray for us
All holy innocents,	pray for us
St Stephen,	pray for us
St Ignatius,	pray for us
St Lawrence,	pray for us
St Vincent,	pray for us
St Fabian and Sebastian,	pray for us
St John and Paul,	pray for us
St Cosmas and Damian,	pray for us
St Gervase and Protasius,	pray for us
All holy martyrs,	pray for us
St Leo,	pray for us
St Gregory,	pray for us
St Ambrose,	pray for us
St Augustine,	pray for us
St Jerome,	pray for us
St Martin,	pray for us

St Nicholas,	pray for us
All holy bishops and confessors,	pray for us
All holy doctors,	pray for us
St Anthony,	pray for us
St Benedict,	pray for us
St Dominic,	pray for us
St Francis,	pray for us
St Ignatius Loyola,	pray for us
St Francis Xavier,	pray for us
St John Vianney,	pray for us
All holy priests,	pray for us
All holy monks and hermits,	pray for us
St Mary Magdalen,	pray for us
St Agatha,	pray for us
St Lucy,	pray for us
St Agnes,	pray for us
St Cecilia,	pray for us
St Catherine,	pray for us
St Anastasia,	pray for us
St Teresa,	pray for us
St George,	pray for us
St David,	pray for us
St Patrick,	pray for us
All holy virgins and widows,	pray for us
All holy saints of God,	make intercession for us
Lamb of God, you take away the sins of the world,	spare us, O Lord
Lamb of God, you take away the sins of the world,	graciously hear us, O Lord
Lamb of God, you take away the sins of the world,	have mercy on us

God our Father, your nature is always to have mercy: receive our
petitions that we and all your children may through your compassion
and goodness be cleansed from our sins and attain to eternal salvation;
through Christ our Lord.

Index of Prayers

Basic prayers

Morning

O my God, I believe in you, 23
Open our hearts, O Lord, and enlighten us, 25
Set our hearts on fire, 29
What return can I make, 23

During the day

Almighty God, the giver of all good things, 31
Blessed Lord, by your life at Nazareth, 33
Father of all that is good, 33
Father of all mankind, 33
O Christ, you are continually worshipped in heaven, 34
O come, Holy Spirit, and inflame my heart, 32
O God, the protector of all who trust in you, 33
O Holy Spirit, giver of light and life, 32
Take not your Holy Spirit from me, 31
Teach us, gracious Lord, 33

At table

Bless, Lord, this food you give us, 34
Bless, O Lord, this food and ourselves, 34
Bless us, O Lord, and these your gifts, 34
We give you thanks, almighty God, for these, 34

At evening and night-time

Abba, Father, the world is so quiet, 44
Almighty Father, who covers the earth, 41
Be present, O merciful God, and protect us, 42
Bless, O Lord, my parents, family and friends, 40
Come, my Light, and illumine my darkness, 37
Eternal Light, shine into our hearts, 37
God be in my head, 43
Grant, O Lord God, that we may cleave, 42
Guard us, O Lord, as the apple of your eye, 45
Hail gladdening Light, of his pure glory poured, 36
Holy Spirit, I thank you for the quiet moments of this busy day, 36
I confess to almighty God, 44
Into your hands, O Lord, I commend my spirit, 46
Into your hands, our Lord and Father, 41

For general use

In doubt and uncertainty

For repentance and renewal

For other people

Almighty and eternal God, may your grace enkindle, 78
Blessed Lord, you have commanded, 78
Christ has no body now on earth but yours, 79
Lord Jesus Christ, good shepherd of the sheep, 78
Lord, we pray for the power to be gentle, 79
Make us worthy, Lord, to serve, 79
We beg you, Lord, to help and defend us, 78

For getting on with others

Almighty God, have mercy on all who bear me evil will, 54
Dear God, help me to be human, 53
From the cowardice, 54
Give us a sense of humour, Lord, 53
Give us, Lord, a humble spirit, 53
God grant me the serenity, 53
God of love, you have given us, 52
God our Father, direct our ways, 52
Heavenly Father, in your wisdom, 53
Lord Jesus, teach us how to be humble, 52
Lord Jesus, you have taught us that love, 77
Lord Jesus, you have taught us that we can only be forgiven, 52
O God, you have bound us together, 54
O Lord, we know that we very often worry, 54

Prayers of blessing

Bless all who worship you, almighty God, 85
Bless this house, O Lord, and all who live in it, 86
Have mercy on me, O God, according to your steadfast love, 87
Lord, in your mercy, give us living water, 87
May God, the Lord, bless us and make us pure, 85
May the Father of heaven grant us from the riches of his glory, 85
O God, make the door of this house wide enough, 86
The grace of our Lord Jesus Christ, 85
This water reminds us of our baptism, 87
We commend ourselves to God's gracious mercy, 85

Before a journey

To the Holy Spirit

Mass and Holy Communion

Before the Blessed Sacrament

Sacrament of Reconciliation and preparation for Confession

In sickness and suffering

For the dying and departed

The Blessed Virgin Mary

Saints

For work

For study and examinations

For school

For the start of term

At the end of term

For sport

For a choir

Before serving Mass

After serving Mass

For the future and for vocations

For the Pope

Almighty and eternal God, have mercy, 79

For the Church

Most glorious and most bountiful God, 80
O God of unchangeable power, 80

For the Queen

Almighty God, whose kingdom is everlasting, 80

For the government

Sovereign Master, you have given authority, 81

For world peace

Almighty God, from whom all thoughts, 80

For benefactors

Almighty God, your desire, 81
God our Father, you inspired, 81
Lord God, the glory of all the faithful, 130
Pour out your love on our family, 81

Fridays

Blessed Saviour, who at this hour hung on the Cross, 84
Lord, in answer to our prayer, 84
Lord Jesus, as you set out on the way of the Cross, 83
Lord Jesus, as we look on the Cross, 84
Lord Jesus, you gave your life, 83

Saturdays

Bless us, Father of all creation, 84
Heavenly Father, as you filled Mary with grace, 84

Advent

Christmas

New Year

Lent

Holy Week

Easter

Ascension

Pentecost

The Stations of the Cross,

Litanies

Acknowledgements

A Note from the Editor

Our first lessons in faith and prayer are learnt at our parents' knees, and in the first place I would like to acknowledge my debt to my own mother and father, who taught me my first prayers and to use my first prayerbook as a child. That is how I began to pray on my own. I cannot thank them enough for that.

I would also like to express my thanks to Abbot Charles Fitzgerald Lombard, for his advice and comment in the preparation of this book. He and Dom Laurence Kelly have been responsible for previous editions of the Downside Prayerbook, to which I hope this volume will be a worthy successor. Dom Antony Sutch, the Head Master, has been from the outset a driving force behind the work which has been done, and also a much appreciated source of encouragement. The present book could never have been composed without the dedication of Mr David Ackerman, to whom I owe a special debt of gratitude not only for his work on the text, but also for the excitement and enjoyment we have been able to share in bringing its contents together. David has undertaken much of the hard work involved in preparing the book for publication in conjunction with Mr Stratford Caldecott of T&T Clark.

The interest and support of boys at Downside School has also meant a great deal: a number of prayers were offered for consideration and these have been included as far as possible.

The editor and publisher gratefully acknowledge permission to reproduce copyright material in this book. Whilst every effort has been made to trace the owners of copyright material, apologies are offered if copyright has been infringed and amendments will, of course, be made in future editions. We are grateful to:

Ampleforth Abbey Trustees for permission to reproduce the prayers for monastic vocations from St Benedict's Prayer Book for Beginners 1993; Brother Bernard SSF for permission to reproduce the prayer 'Lord, I want to love you, yet I'm not sure'; Continuum Publishing for permission to reproduce 'Lord, give us grace to hold to you' from *The Face of Love* by Gilbert Shaw, 'Come, my light, and illuminate my darkness' from *The Orthodox Way* by Kallistos Ware (published by Mowbray, an imprint of Continuum), and the prayers 'For a sick child' and 'Father, your son accepted', from the *Pastoral Care of the Sick* (published by Geoffrey Chapman, an imprint of Continuum); The Church Mission Society for permission to reproduce the Kenyan prayer published in J. Carden, *Morning Noon and Night*, 1976; Darton Longman & Todd Ltd and Doubleday & Co for permission to reproduce verses from the *New Jerusalem Bible*, published and copyright 1985; Faber & Faber for permission to reproduce the prayer 'Thou who art over us' from *Markings* by Dag Hammarskjöld (translated by Leif Sjoberg and W. H. Auden); Franciscan Herald Press for permission to reproduce the Prayer to Our Lady by St Francis from *Omnibus of Sources: Early Writings and Early Biographies*, ed. Marion A. Habig OFM; Friends of York Minster for permission to reproduce 'My God and Father' from *My God, My Glory* by Eric Milner-White; Harper Collins for permission to reproduce 'Lord God, our loving Father' from *Jesus Christ the Way, the Truth and the Life*, by David Konstant; Hodder & Stoughton for permissiion to reproduce 'Holy Spirit, I thank you for the quiet moments' from the *Treasury of the Holy Spirit* ed. Mgr Michael Buckley; The Lutterworth Press for permission to reproduce 'O Lord, you know we very often worry' from *Prayers at Breakfast* by Beryl Bye; McCrimmon Publishing Co Ltd, 10–12 High Street, Great Wakering, Essex SS3 OEQ, for permission to reproduce the Rite of Confession, 'Greeting', 'Confession of Sins', and 'Act of Contrition', from the *Penitent's Prayer Book*, compiled by David Konstant, and 'Give us a sense of humour, Lord', 'Lord Jesus, you have taught us', 'God grant me the serenity', 'Lord Jesus, teach us how to be humble', 'O God, you have bound us together', 'Almighty God, who covers the earth', 'Lord, I believe in you', from *The One Who Listens* by Michael Hollings and Etta Gullick; Oxford University Press for permission to reproduce 'Eternal Father of my soul' from *A Diary of Private Prayer* by John Baillie, 1936 and 'O Holy Spirit, giver of light and life', 'Lord Jesus, you have taught us', 'Heavenly Father, in your wisdom' and 'God our Father, in your generosity' from *Daily Prayer* by Eric Milner-White and G. W. Briggs, 1941; Redemptorist Publications for permission to reproduce prayers from the *Pope John Sunday Missal*; SCM Press Ltd for permission to reproduce 'O Lord my God, thank you' and 'O God, early in the morning I cry to you' from 'Prayers for Fellow Prisoners' from *Letters and Papers from Prison*, the Enlarged Edition, by Dietrich Bonhoeffer, 1971, pp. 139–142; SPCK for permission to reproduce 'O God, I thank you for life and being' and for permission to adapt 'O Lord we pray thee' from *One Man's Prayers* by George Appleton, 1967.

The 'Prayer to St Joseph' is reproduced from *Prayers to Our Lady and the Saints* by courtesy of Catholic Truth Society, London; the prayer 'Before an exam' is reproduced with the permission of Mrs B. E. Salmon, Trust House, Veryan, Truro, Cornwall TR2 5QA; the Post Communion collects 'Almighty God, we thank you for feeding us' and 'Father of all, we give you thanks and praise' from the Alternative Service book 1980 and copyright ©The Central Board of Finance of the Church of England and are reproduced by permission; 'Thankyou, Lord, for the pleasure of sport' is reproduced from *The Lion Christian Prayer Book* by Mary Batchelor with the permission of William Neill-Hall Ltd; the poem 'Godhead here in hiding' which is a translation of the Latin hymn *Adoro te devote* is taken from *The Poems of Gerard Manley Hopkins* (4th ed. 1967) ed. W. H. Gardner and N. H. Mackenzie ©The Society of Jesus and is reproduced by permission of Oxford University Press; the prayer 'Father, we thank you for your blessing on this school' is based on a prayer of King's College, Cambridge; the prayer 'Almighty God, our Heavenly Father, we commend to your care' (in the Downside School supplement) is based on a prayer of Westminster College, Oxford and has been adapted with permission; New Testament canticles (Magnificat, Nunc Dimittis) and extracts from Psalms 51 and 130, Galatians, Philippians and 1 Peter are from the New Revised Standard Version Bible, copyright © 1989 by the Division of Christian Education of the National Council of the Churches of Christ in the USA, and are used by permission. All rights reserved.

Adapted extracts from The Book of Common Prayer, the rights in which are vested in the Crown, are reproduced by permission of the Crown's Patentee, Cambridge University Press.

In most cases the style of language used in prayers in this book has been modernized. This has meant that slight alterations to a prayer's structure have sometimes been made. Although the author's name below a prayer indicates no substantial changes have been made, 'thee' and 'thine', etc. will have been replaced by 'you' and 'your', and this may have necessitated some structural adjustments.

Sources of prayers believed to be in the public domain are: *A Manual of Catholic Prayer*, Burns & Oates, an imprint of Continuum, 1962; *A Manual* of *Catholic Devotion*, The Church Literature Association, 1950; *A Chain of Prayers Across the Centuries*, John Murray, compiled by Selina Fitzherbert Fox, first published 1913; *Catholic Prayers for Church of England People*, W. Knott & Son, 1959.

Where unattributed, prayers are either composed by the editors or are believed to be traditional.